The High-Performing

The High-Performing Preschool
Story Acting in Head Start Classrooms

Gillian Dowley McNamee

The University of Chicago Press
Chicago and London

Gillian Dowley McNamee is professor of child development
and director of teacher education at the Erikson Institute
in Chicago. She is coauthor of *Early Literacy, The Fifth
Dimension: An After School Program Built on Diversity*, and
*Bridging: Assessment for Teaching and Learning in Early
Childhood Classrooms*.

The University of Chicago Press, Chicago 60637
The University of Chicago Press, Ltd., London
© 2015 by The University of Chicago
All rights reserved. Published 2015.
Printed in the United States of America

24 23 22 21 20 19 18 17 16 15   1 2 3 4 5

ISBN-13: 978-0-226-26081-5 (cloth)
ISBN-13: 978-0-226-26095-2 (paper)
ISBN-13: 978-0-226-26100-3 (e-book)
DOI: 10.7208/chicago/9780226261003.001.0001

Library of Congress Cataloging-in-Publication Data

McNamee, Gillian Dowley, 1951– author.
  The high-performing preschool: story acting in Head Start
classrooms / Gillian Dowley McNamee.
    pages; cm
  Includes bibliographical references and index.
  ISBN 978-0-226-26081-5 (cloth: alk. paper) — ISBN 0-226-
26081-X (cloth: alk. paper) — ISBN 978-0-226-26095-2
(pbk.: alk. paper) — ISBN 0-226-26095-X (pbk.: alk.
paper) — ISBN 978-0-226-26100-3 (e-book) 1. Storytelling
in education. 2. Education, Preschool—Activity programs.
3. Head Start programs. 4. Vygotskii, L. S. (Lev Semenovich),
1896–1934. 5. Paley, Vivian Gussin, 1929– I. Title.
  LB1042.M36 2015
  372.67'7—dc23   2014040937

♾ This paper meets the requirements of ANSI/NISO
Z39.48-1992 (Permanence of Paper).

For my storytellers,
Michael, Nicole, and Jamie

Contents

Foreword
Michael Cole

The book you are about to read represents the meeting of a remark-able, and remarkably practical, American preschool teacher, Vivian Gussin Paley, with Lev Semyonovich Vygotsky, a highly theoreti-cal Russian developmental psychologist who died when Paley was herself a preschooler. The medium for this unusual confluence of classroom teacher and research scholar is Gillian Dowley McNa-mee, and the question she is asking through Paley and Vygotsky is one that has been plaguing American education for decades:

What are the sources of difficulty in school for young children, especially children of the poor and most especially children of color, and how might their academic achievement difficulties be erased through more effective educational practices?

• • •

I first met Gillian Dowley when I was a young professor and she was a beginning researcher in a Head Start program in Central Harlem. Gillian and I were taking a close look at a phenomenon highlighted in the research by sociolinguist William Labov. Labov had reported a compelling case study illustrating stark contrasts between the way that poor, black school-age children use language in school with the way that they use it at home and in their neighborhoods. Con-troversial prior research described children of poverty, and particularly black children living in poverty, as culturally and linguistically deprived. If they had developed language at all, they had failed to develop it as a tool of thought.

Labov showed, however, that a monosyllabic child in a standardized psychological test situation could be transformed into a voluble, expressive, rhetorician outside of school when accompanied by a friend, snacking on popcorn, and talking informally about neighborhood and family events. We wanted to replicate Labov's results and to explore how they might manifest themselves in preschoolers attending Head Start.

Over several years, we worked in collaboration with teachers in a Head Start program in central Harlem. One sign of the trust in which we were held is that Miss Gil, as she was called, was given permission to take the children, two at a time, to the local supermarket. The children made the trip in a shopping cart. They were each allowed to buy a piece of fruit to take back to the classroom for snack time. In the shopping cart with the pairs of three- and four-year-olds was a tape recorder. When they returned to the classroom, the children were asked to recount their experiences at the supermarket and to share the food that they had bought. We had a tape recorder present for that event too.

We then compared the children's conversations during the supermarket outing to those with their teachers and peers in the classroom. In one respect our data replicated perfectly what Labov had reported. The amount and complexity of the children's talk was significantly greater in the supermarket than in the classroom.

We then looked more closely to see what kind of speech occurred in the two settings. We found that in the supermarket, the most frequent verbalizations by children were descriptions of what they were seeing and doing as they negotiated what to buy. However, in the classroom, the children's talk was dominated by responses to yes/no questions or other teacher comments that limited the child's choices in how to respond. When we focused only on those occasions when the children described or commented on some aspect of their experiences, the complexity of their talk in the classroom was equal to that in the supermarket. So how could we create conditions in the classroom where children felt encouraged to speak freely, even though they were more likely to be on the receiving end of a lot of questions?

As we and Labov found, the children clearly did not lack language skills. But our results made it clear that the activities taking place as a part of institutionalized schooling have their own "academic" form of language and ways of doing things. Children must not only expand their vocabularies but also be very adept at responding to "known-answer questions," such as "What color is this triangle?" or "What shape is this ball?" If children arrive at school without understanding how to engage in this form of discourse and the special literacy and numeracy skills at its heart, how do we arrange for them to master it? This is the question at the heart of Gillian's book, the life work of her mentor Vivian Paley, and much of Lev Vygotsky's research.

Vygotsky enters this story through his ideas about the role of play in children's intellectual development. As Gillian notes in her introduction, her time conducting research at the Laboratory of Comparative Human Cognition coincided with the period when we were all reading draft translations of the work of Lev Vygotsky that would be published a few years later. We were very excited about his idea that play creates a "zone of proximal development" during early childhood. The zone of proximal development, or ZPD, is formally defined as the difference between what learners can accomplish independently and what they can achieve with help. A good teacher discerns what parts of a task children can do, and then builds upon their budding abilities to help them grow, tapering off his or her involvement as the child moves toward independent mastery. We were excited by the possibility that understanding how zones of proximal development work might transform our understanding of learning and play among three- and four-year-olds in Head Start. For Vygotsky, play is symbolic; it is verbal, social, and cultural—all features of language and thinking we were seeking to integrate in educating Head Start children.

We had the chance to pursue one more step in this inquiry. We chose to replicate a study by Zenaida Istomina, a student of Aleksei Leont'ev, who was himself a pupil and colleague of Vygotsky's. Istomina compared three- to seven-year-old children's memories of a set of common grocery-store items in two circumstances. In the first, the memory task was embedded in the game of "going to the store," a typical play activity of this preschool. In the second, the children were presented the same items in a more straightforward memory task. During the preschool period, children remembered significantly more when the task was a part of their familiar game than when it was presented as an assignment from their teacher.

When we sought to replicate this experiment with Head Start children in their classroom, we failed to find any difference between the two conditions. Why? Because, despite our best efforts, we failed to create two qualitatively different circumstances for remembering. No play occurred in either. Our children approached both tasks as if they were assignments—they were following directions. To invert a well-known phrase from Vivian Paley's work, we had learned the hard way that you can't say "You *must* play." It won't happen. The command takes all the fun out of play, so to speak. We were stymied. How could we incorporate play into settings where adults set the agenda for what children are supposed to do?

Gillian's answer came when she met Vivian Paley in her kindergarten classroom at the University of Chicago Laboratory Schools. It was not long before I began to hear a lot about Vivian Paley and the many ways that pretend play was giving rise to zones of proximal development all over her classroom. Gillian was thrilled to see that Vivian's teaching practices bore an uncanny resemblance to the ideas of Vygotsky that we had been studying at the Lab.

It is now almost four decades since Gillian set out for Chicago. Gillian is now professor and director of teacher education at the Erikson Institute, a graduate school in child development. She is teaching a new generation of early childhood educators. She works with student teachers and travels to different Head Start classrooms in the economically deprived areas of Chicago, supporting teachers in listening to their children. This book is based on a year of visits to the classrooms where Gillian used the work of Lev Vygotsky and Vivian Paley to show how all kinds of children can benefit from learning through storytelling and story acting.

The efficacy of Vivian Paley's preschool play with storytelling and story-acting pedagogy supports the following conclusion: The

Paley preschool curriculum (only part of which, it must be emphasized, is devoted to her story-dictation-enactment practices) provides a comprehensive curriculum *and* method of teaching that
encompasses all children in learning. It is both comprehensive and
inclusive. It not only provides an excellent, integrated preparation
for the literacy and numeracy challenges that await in kindergarten
and first grade, it does so in a manner that meets the Common Core
State Standards that are currently the subject of heated debate in
this country.

If this conclusion is correct, it leaves us, the readers, with three
questions.

1. How does the Paley curriculum work when it is properly imple-
    mented? What replicable processes are involved?
2. What are the difficulties in implementation? Does it require a
    uniquely talented teacher, or can it be implemented by ordinary
    mortals? And can even an extraordinary teacher implement it in a
    classroom that is organized around direct instruction in the pre-
    sumed subskills of reading: phonemic awareness, phonics, vocabu-
    lary, fluency, and comprehension?
3. If implementation is possible, and ordinary teachers can learn to
    implement it, what policies need to be adopted to see that the curric-
    ulum is made widely available?

My answers to each of these questions is based on my reading of
the evidence that emerges from Gillian's lucid account.

How Does the Paley Curriculum Work?

I have long been enamored of the metaphor of culture as a garden, inspired by Raymond Williams's observation that in all of its
early uses, the term *culture* referred to the process of helping things
grow—a perfect starting point for a developmental psychologist.
So it has always tickled my fancy that in reading Vygotsky's ideas
about play and development, Gillian focused on his use of the garden metaphor as a way to explain the much-debated idea of a zone
of proximal development. As Vygotsky phrased it, a zone of proxi-

mal development "defines those functions that are not mature yet, but are currently in the process of maturation, the functions that will mature tomorrow. These functions are not fruits yet, but buds or flowers of development" (1978, 86). A good teacher, like a good gardener, Gillian writes, must be able to discern the earliest stages of the child's developing capacities well before they are visible to the untrained eye, and to nurture them appropriately.

Just as a bean seed looks little like the fruit that grows after the seed has transformed into the plant and the plant has developed flowers, Gillian tells us that in literacy development, the process of learning to read and write begins in activities that do not necessarily look like their mature forms. She illustrates this process of identifying "buds" and nurturing the process of development in seemingly simple terms, beginning with observing the origins of a story in a child's pretend play. Just how different the seed of a story can be from its mature form, and how deftly the teacher must identify and nurture it, can be pretty amazing.

Having spotted such a story seed, the teacher asks the child to dictate it and quickly writes it down in preparation for acting it out with other children at the first appropriate moment. When that moment comes, the child is invited to act out the story along with other children who take on the additional roles that the story requires.

The first thing to note is that children's fantasy play is only the starting point in the process. As Gillian explains, in the act of dictation, the child's imagination is momentarily diverted from play into a printed story.

Second, by using fantasy play as a starting point for story dictation, the process of bringing a child's ideas to the community for consideration emerges from, and embodies, the child's own interests and intentions. As the work of developmental psychologist Michael Tomasello and others have shown, adult talk that follows through on children's intentions is an optimal procedure for promoting language development. (And as Gillian's earlier work on preschoolers' communications in supermarkets versus the classroom established, children's language expression is most complex when they are initiating the conversation.)

Third, when the teacher reads the story aloud for the group and the children enact it, the process that Gillian singles out for close scrutiny in this book, dramatization, comes into play (pun intended). As Vygotsky would explain it, this is the moment when the thinking of the individual meets that of the collective, the classroom community, and the story is opened up for examination, understanding, and future adaptation. This is the piece of the learning sequence that any of us might pass over too quickly if Vygotsky had not pointed out its significance—the interplay of one's ideas with that of the group. Dramatization, if viewed through Vygotsky's framework, is the high road to Head Start children becoming verbally fluent *in school* and in school discourse patterns.

Finally, we can see that in the transitions from play to dictation to enacting, the children are engaging in a process developmental psychologist Annette Karmiloff-Smith calls "re-representation," in which the same ideas are formulated and expressed linguistically in a new way—in this case, through improvisational acting. I can imagine that Vygotsky would have particularly liked this line of theorizing because, in his words, "The acquisition of language can provide a paradigm for the entire problem of the relation between learning and development" (1978, 89).

But to be effective, it appears essential that these individual dramatization sequences be integrated into the daily routines of the classroom; a peer culture of storytelling and collective enactment must be formed, as developmental psychologist Ageliki Nicolopoulou has emphasized. From this perspective, the prospect of acting out their own stories, along with peers, is a powerful motive for children to compose stories. The public, peer-oriented nature of the activity creates what she calls a "community of storytellers" that makes children eager to participate. The thinking of the individual is given a safe and respectful opportunity to be influenced by the community. We have in hand the development of the young child's "mind in society."

In sum, we have a pretty strong idea of what psychological processes are brought into alignment to produce a virtuous cycle of learning and development for preschoolers in Mrs. Paley's classroom and in Head Start. Properly implemented, the Paley dramatization curriculum works because it ensures that the tools of literacy and numeracy arise as means to achieving ends that the children are pursuing both individually and collectively.

What Are the Difficulties of Implementation?

With this grasp on the processes that underpin successful engagement in Vivian Paley's curriculum that is centered around dramatization, we can address the second key question: If it works when properly implemented, under what conditions can such transformative events be organized as a central part of a preschool classroom's culture?

As Gillian describes, effectively implementing dramatization activities in normal Head Start classrooms can be difficult. This caution echoes strongly in research that has sought to implement the curriculum with teachers who have encountered Mrs. Paley only in her books, many of whom work in schools and classrooms that are very focused on direct instruction of skills.

Gillian's account of her experiences in Head Start classrooms provides many examples of the kinds of challenges that teachers face when implementing the dramatization, challenges that have also been identified in research seeking to introduce this mode of teaching on a larger scale. First, of course, teachers must develop a keen eye for spotting incipient stories. Then they must create opportunities for the children to experiment on their own, offering guidance in developing their narrative skills and providing new storylines from classical children's literature for children to draw upon.

Next, teachers are confronted with challenges in classroom management as they strive to balance individual children's concerns while simultaneously considering the needs of the whole group. Dramatization is only one of many activities taking place in the classroom, so teachers must also be able to create structured routines such that transitions from one activity to the next occur with little disruption. Children excited by the group dramatizations do not easily settle down for the next, quieter activity. A skilled practitioner can collect dictated stories in a few minutes or less, but even with an assistant teacher to help out, a good deal of improvisational balancing is a constant part of the effective teacher's repertoire of techniques for implementing dramatization.

Perhaps one of Gillian's most significant achievements in *The High-Performing Preschool: Story Acting in Head Start Classrooms* is that she demonstrates that the Head Start teachers she visits and works among acquire the necessary skills for including the dramatization curriculum within their daily routines. She offers critical insight into how the challenges with dramatization can in fact be an opportunity to examine the components of effective teaching of young children. Research in education, child development, and language learning attest to the need for children to participate in active, ongoing, literacy-rich conversations in the classroom to develop narrative skills about what is not present in the immediate here and now. That is exactly what the storytelling and story-acting activities accomplish. They provide an unusual opportunity for combining fantasy play with structured examination of ideas by children in small- and large-group discussions. Gillian demonstrates that the Paley curriculum does not require rare pedagogical genius or years of specialized instruction in college classrooms. Given proper support, all teachers can implement it.

What Policies Are Needed to Ensure That the Curriculum Is Made Widely Available?

Here we arrive at what is perhaps the most difficult question of all. Gillian's account of her year visiting Head Start classrooms strongly suggests that her periodic presence provides local teachers with a working model that they can adapt to their own practices. This kind of ongoing in situ support requires mentors with the skills and resolve to be there for the teachers. Such support is not a free good. It requires investment in teacher training as well as support for well-trained mentoring teachers. That's all—along with paper, pencils, and a good collection of high-quality children's literature.

The combined voices of Mrs. Paley and Professor Vygotsky urge us to seriously consider the enormous potential of a dramatization curriculum to provide all young children, regardless of their home backgrounds, a real head start in the serious business of equipping themselves for adult life. An investment is needed in teachers who understand how to engage children's imagination in school—with one another, and with teachers who ask, "What story do you have to tell? I want to hear yours, and I have great ones to read to you. Together, we will make school an exciting place to be." Gillian Dowley McNamee shows how Head Start can launch children's public school education in a way that will draw them in for years to come.

Preface

It's early November and Mrs. Ashford is driving her four-year-old granddaughter, Daniella, to school. Potholes lacing the quiet street of row houses, many with boarded-up windows, make the driving slow. Green Park Elementary School, a large, 1920s redbrick building, sits uncrowded by a vacant lot, an unpaved parking lot, and a fenced-in playground often sprinkled with broken glass. They arrive at Carol Miller's Head Start classroom, and as Daniella hangs up her coat, scarf, and hat, she calls out, "Teacher! I'm going to tell a story about a angel today. My mama say I a angel." Mrs. Miller replies, "Hi, Daniella. Hi, Mrs. Ashford! Come have breakfast, Daniella. Then we'll write down your story." Daniella continues as she sits down, "There gonna be seven angels in my story. It gotta be girls."

Daniella is already anticipating the end of the morning, when the class will act out stories that the children have dictated to their teachers. The author can play whichever character she wants in her story, while the teacher invites children from around the edge of the rug to assume other roles in the dramatization. This enacts an ethic of inclusion in the classroom: anyone can play any part in the reenactment of ideas, and must be given an equal opportunity to do so. Daniella is lobbying for special dispensation from this class rule. She envisions a scene of seven angels, a posse of girls in their element, perhaps like the twelve dancing princesses in the Grimm's fairy tale that Mrs. Miller recently read to them.

After breakfast, Mrs. Miller picks up her notebook and calls, "Daniella, I'm ready for that story now. How does your angel story begin?" Daniella runs over to the table, where Mrs. Miller pulls out two chairs. Daniella settles in, her head leaning over the page where her teacher is ready to write each word she says. She dictates in phrases, her eyes tracking every movement of her teacher's pen; Mrs. Miller echoes each word as Daniella offers it.

> Once upon a time there were seven little angels. They lived in a castle. And then the seven little angels bring their little cousin to play. They play with their cousin. They play jump rope and hopscotch. Then they saw their mother. They see their grandpa, and uncle, and cousin. They all have a family angel meeting. They eat popcorn and watch a movie. All done!

Daniella heads off to the art table to make a crown out of pipe cleaners. Four other children dictate stories, portraying mothers, babies, dragons, and other characters facing and overcoming dangers.

Later in the morning when the class gathers around the edge of the rug, Mrs. Miller announces that it is time to act out stories. "Daniella, your story is first." Daniella jumps up, saying to the girls next to her, "Come on, you're in this story. The angels gotta be girls!" The girls are on their feet and very quickly there is a group in the middle of the rug. One girl is absent today, so the numbers come out right. Mrs. Miller announces to the group: "There are seven angels in Daniella's story. Let's count." They do a quick count and the girls beam, happy to be named an angel.

The teacher then calls for a little cousin, grandpa, and uncle. Starting with the boy on her right, she proceeds around the circle recruiting actors. "Do you want to be the cousin?" When she sees a head nod, she says, "Good, come onto the stage." Pointing to the next child, she asks, "Will you be the grandpa? *Abuelo*?" When the child shakes his head no, she moves to the next child. Recruiting a mother is slightly more difficult; several boys do not want that role.

Finally, one agrees to play the mother because being a part of the growing swarm of children on the stage is more appealing than sitting on the sidelines. Fifteen children are present in school that day, and eleven are acting in the story. The rug is crowded and the image of each character is a bit blurred as the angels float about pretending to jump rope and play hopscotch.

Daniella's story is shaped by personal images of happiness, but its dramatization at group time gives it new significance. The gathering of children on the rug is the affirmation of a new meaning that her story can have in school. In storytelling and story acting, children and teachers come together as a community in ways that complement, reinforce, and expand a child's personal fantasies. Eating popcorn and watching a movie together in this pretend story spells togetherness, friendship, and comfort in her story and in the classroom.

This set of activities integrated into Daniella's day, including dictation of a story that she later acts out at group time with classmates, is part of a carefully planned curricular intervention for this Head Start classroom. Its blueprint derives from the work of early twentieth-century Russian psychologist Lev Vygotsky and early childhood education teacher and writer Vivian G. Paley. Their ideas guide this discussion of the most urgent educational challenges for our nation's youngest public school children: How can classroom teachers enhance the oral-language foundations of children who are growing up in communities experiencing economic hardship, with different backgrounds in language, dialect, and cultural traditions? What curricular approach will initiate them into active verbal participation in a community of learners ready for the full breadth of educational opportunities school has to offer?

One way to close the academic-achievement gap of children from low-income families is to familiarize them with the kinds of experiences and concomitant vocabulary of their middle-class peers, and with the discourse patterns that school presupposes for large groups of children with teachers. Head Start teachers orient young children to the conventions of classroom conversations about a broad range of topics connected to literature, mathematics, social studies, the sciences, and the arts. Listening to read-alouds in a large group is a brand-new experience for children, as is learning to discuss their ideas.

Furthermore, school is built around dialogue patterns that Courtney Cazden first described as initiation-response-evaluation (2001, 29). Teachers ask a question that invites a child's response, which the teacher then evaluates as correct or incorrect.

> TEACHER: How many girls are in school today?
> DANIELLA: Seven.
> TEACHER: Right. Now we are ready.

Such responses are not in keeping with everyday conversational expectations. Why are teachers asking questions they already know the answer to, and why are they evaluating the accuracy of a child's almost every utterance? Educators have come to recognize that children who are not from the mainstream middle-class culture do not automatically recognize, understand, and adjust to expectations of school that are foreign to them in many ways. What do Vygotsky and Mrs. Paley have to offer children and their teachers about learning the ways of school?

The writings of Vivian Paley describe stories that her children tell and later act out in impromptu dramatizations during the school day as the anchor to the verbally rich, creative learning in her classroom. When we step back to consider what children gain from this experience, we begin to realize that she found the cornerstone to school learning: narrative uses of language about both imaginary and real-life experiences. Learning in school requires children to listen carefully, and to use words to create and make sense of experiences, most of which are not present in the here and now but are accessed through spoken and printed words. Mrs. Paley helps us see that the first steps toward such language use are best cultivated in teaching children to engage in pretend play and giving them a forum to tell stories and act them out.

Vygotsky's essays in *Mind in Society* (1978) underscore the significance of Vivian Paley's work. Vygotsky was the first psychologist to develop a theoretical framework for describing the process of a child's mental development without reducing the variables to one-on-one interactions. He was intrigued with groups and sought to explain the development of the individual in relation to community settings. This is exactly the kind of theory that is needed to explain teaching and learning in school. School has always organized learning for groups of children with a teacher. Educators tend to emphasize and try to account for the primacy of the teacher in a child's learning, portraying it as the product of a one-way relationship. However, in the presence of good teaching, the equation of learning is more complex. What happens to and with other children in the classroom matters. Each child's learning becomes everyone else's business.

Without having ever heard of Vygotsky in her early work, Vivian Paley's writings offered rich examples of young minds developing *in* society. The storytelling and story-acting activities illustrate the fundamental equation of learning in school: that it is not dyadic, or exclusively between adult and child. Rather, learning is situated between each child and the group that includes the teacher and the child's peers. Mrs. Paley provides the best examples available in educational literature of a teacher organizing the school day so that children speak, listen, and participate in creating a unique literary community. A master at understanding the dynamics involved in the interaction of the group with each individual child's learning, Mrs. Paley offers rich documentation of children's learning alongside peers in her thirteen published books.

From a Vygotskian perspective, literacy is not an individual achievement but a social one, a societal one. How teachers use words, both written and spoken, to mediate the building of relationships in the classroom community is essential to the young child's long-term motivation to come to school, listen carefully to others, and read and write about their own thinking and that of others. How teachers guide children in listening to and telling their stories in a fair and inclusive school community determines the footing, or lack of it, that children gain when they enter classrooms.

Mrs. Miller's interactions with Daniella around her angel story illustrate the core of Vivian Paley's curriculum: acting out stories authored by the children themselves. The dictation and dramatization of the children's stories alongside those that the teachers select to read to the class provide a unique opportunity to study the core dynamics of school: both one-on-one interactions between teacher and child, and the intersection of the child's thinking with that of their peer group. Vygotsky would say that the opportunity for Daniella and her classmates to dictate and act out stories with classmates enacts the goals of schooling. The children are being inducted into a literary community through their stories, conversations, and play. They experience the power of both connecting with and expanding one another's thinking through words alone: spoken, written, and enacted.

The chapters that follow explore this part of teaching, which depends on what children are learning from their teacher and from one another. How and why are other children, whether rich or poor, an essential part of each child's learning in school? What is a teacher's role in organizing the class so that the collective provides the strength and resources for each child to achieve their potential every day of the school year?

Studying Learning in School

As an early childhood teacher educator, I spend time in public school classrooms with student teachers and with teachers with whom the Erikson Institute has a professional development partnership. I carry with me a notebook and pencil to write down children's dictated stories. I also carry in my memory other favorite stories plus dozens of songs and nursery rhymes I can call upon when a teacher asks me to take the group while he or she attends to a message or parent who has arrived needing immediate attention.

The activities of "doing stories"—as a child described it to Mrs. Paley when she visited another classroom (2001, 3)—are basic teaching activities that I practice whenever I get a chance. They provide an entrée into the intellectual life of young children at any moment and help build a connection between the teacher's thinking and that of the children. My readiness to engage children with these few resources also gives teachers a chance to observe their students; it also allows me to assist a student teacher who wants to learn alongside a more experienced mentor. Later we compare notes on what they observed about their children's interactions with another teacher.

Such sustained working relationships with working and aspiring teachers allow me to hone my classroom teaching skills and remain current with teaching today's children. It is also a good basis for partnership teaching—offering teachers and myself the opportunity to discuss the many challenges in daily teaching. These conversations inform the narrative of this book and reflect the kind of dialogues that are critical to teachers' continued professional support and education.

Mrs. Miller has been teaching for seven years, five of them in kindergarten, and she is now in her third year in Head Start. When I told her I wished to study the acting out of stories in Head Start, she willingly agreed to my request to work alongside her and her assistant, Patricia Ortiz, to try out the activities with her children when I visited the school during the year.

Mrs. Miller and her colleagues teach in an urban public school in a community beset with economic hardships. The teachers are working under accountability pressures faced by all public school teachers, where their own performance as well as that of their children is assessed in frequent standardized testing protocols. Even as they face such pressures, these teachers are committed to discussing their work in weekly grade-level meetings and allocated professional development time. We consider how preschool and kindergarten teachers can address the needs as well as the successes of each child in a way that benefits all children. We look for ways that each individual can be noticed and supported in learning by the class throughout the school day.

My long-term goal has been to bring to Head Start classrooms the level of conversation, thinking, and engagement in learning practiced by Mrs. Paley. To date, there have been no sustained and successful pathways for bringing low-income children to high levels of verbal discourse and thinking in school settings. Vivian Paley's books along with Vygotsky's vision for development provide a new way to conceptualize how early childhood education can position all young children for academic achievement, particularly those from culturally different and economically challenged neighborhoods. The story of Mrs. Miller and her children demonstrates that this goal is well within our reach, with the teaching practices needed to achieve the goal at our fingertips. Such practices are not found in expensive commercial curricula; rather, they depend on a rich collection of imaginative quality children's literature, paper and pencil, and a teacher who is prepared to listen, observe, question, and guide children as they explore, invent, and converse about ideas that begin in stories they act out.

The High-Performing Preschool begins with a close examination of Vygotsky and Vivian Paley's scholarship, and how their thinking informs our understanding of the educational needs of all young children entering school, particularly Head Start children. In Chapter 2, we join Mrs. Miller's classroom—along with Vygotsky and Mrs. Paley—where most of the narrative of this book takes place. I situate the challenges Mrs. Miller and her colleagues face in teaching our nation's youngest public-school children within daily classroom activities. I examine the ideas offered by Vygotsky and Mrs. Paley in light of the Common Core State Standards that guide the value and promise of all current educational endeavors in the United States.

Chapters 3, 4, and 5 provide up-close descriptions of Mrs. Miller and myself at work with her Head Start children engaged in the storytelling and story-acting activities that ground the children's learning in the school day. We see the children in action when they are well versed in the activity routines, and then step back to examine what happened in the first days in school when they were first introduced to them. We observe the very first steps the children make with their teacher's guidance, and with Mrs. Paley and Vygotsky watching closely to coach and comment.

Chapter 6 provides a critical piece of the story: the payoff for Head Start children who participate in the storytelling and story-acting activities. Principals and school administrators will encourage and even demand that the storytelling and story activities be carried out in preschool, kindergarten, and the primary grades *if* they are convinced that they will make a critical difference for achieving the high-stakes goals set for all children. In Chapter 6, we visit a school where the activities have been carried out for several years across the preschool through third-grade classrooms. The children's achievements help us gauge how sustained involvement in the story-telling and story-acting activities contributes to learning to read and write while fostering a creative, analytic, thoughtful approach to all school subjects in a way that engenders lifelong learning.

Chapters 7 and 8 shift the focus of discussion from the pre-school children to their teachers and the professional skills they need to effectively implement the storytelling and story-acting ac-tivities. How do these activities fit alongside others in supporting young children's first learning experiences in school, particularly as they relate to talking, reading, and writing? We return to Mrs. Mill-er's classroom, with Vygotsky and Mrs. Paley staying close at hand, guiding the discussion of learning to teach and honing those skills. Professional teaching skills, they help us see, do not come easily or automatically. Careful thinking, discussion, coaching, and support are all required to develop the expertise to guide and assess the learning of young children over time.

Chapter 9 brings us to the last day of school in Mrs. Miller's classroom, where we observe her children in play, storytelling, and story acting to consider how far they have come in meeting the ed-ucational goals set for them. How have they benefited from their Head Start experiences as individuals and as a group?

Both Vygotsky and Mrs. Paley share the belief that children's learning in school is not only about becoming proficient in pre-determined skill sets. Teachers are not the only instructors in the classroom. The development of each child is not a singular enter-prise; it is always plural. Each child's learning has a relationship to others in the classroom, and the children know it. They depend on being able to get their bearings and gauge their progress with the support and insights they readily offer and gather from one another. Vygotsky's theory of the zone of proximal development sets out a path for thinking about the relationships among children and their teachers, which in turn engender the kind of transformative learning that good teaching makes possible. Mrs. Paley provides a portrait of Vygotsky's theory at work and a guide to the practices that are needed for professional teaching of our youngest schoolchildren.

Vygotsky, Vivian Paley, and I are the outsiders entering the community of teachers, children, and families at Green Park Elementary School. While Vygotsky was present always in my thinking, his name never came up in school discussions. The work of Vivian Paley, however, was frequently referred to, as she is well known in early childhood settings. Before we begin, a word about names. In this narrative about Head Start children, I use honorifics with surnames, acknowledging the respect that teachers and administrators accord one another in Green Park Elementary School. Vivian Paley and I become Mrs. Paley and Mrs. McNamee alongside our colleagues who welcomed us in a teaching partnership with them in their Head Start classrooms.

Chapter 1

Zones of Proximal Development in Head Start Classrooms

Mrs. Miller sits with her three- and four-year-old children in front of her on the rug, holding up shapes for them to name and describe. She holds up a green circle and asks in a cheery voice, "What color is this?" Sam calls out, "Brown!" The teacher replies, "What color?" Adrian is eager: "Red!" Mrs. Miller says, "Come on now, look what I am holding. What color is this?" "Blue! Blue!" "No, look at this; this is like the stoplight. It's green. This is a green circle. What is this?" The class responds together, "Green circle." "Good. Now what's this?" the teacher asks as she holds up a red square. A child calls out, "A stoplight!" "No, what color?" "Brown!" "You know this! Come on, what color is this?" Child: "Red!" Mrs. Miller: "Yes, this is a red square! OK, time to go to the tables, and I want you to practice making the letter B. Take your finger and make the letter B in the air with me."

The children do their best to mimic their teacher's motions in the air. They then go off to tables, where they take up pencils that wobble and skitter about in their tiny hands. Their first attempts at letters are about as successful as their color naming. The next day when they come back to the rug, Mrs. Miller reviews the colors of the shapes with them, and then moves on to the names of the shapes. The lessons in shapes, colors, and forming letters occupy much of their school day and present a laborious curriculum challenge for both children and teacher in the weeks and months that follow.

The curriculum will continue with learning the names of the letters of the alphabet, their sounds, recognizing spoken words with the same initial or ending sound, counting the syllables in a word, counting to twenty, and reciting the names of the days of the week and months of the year. With each storybook, they will be taught to name it as "fiction" or "informational," identify the author and illustrator and what work each of them do in writing the book, and they will answer questions about unknown words in the text. Teachers in today's schools are asked to maximize the time spent each day ensuring children's mastery of basic skills and concepts central to school curriculum. The detailing of such knowledge that children are expected to have to be kindergarten ready is growing longer given the goals now identified in the new Common Core State Standards (2010).

Mrs. Miller has been criticized by school administrators at Green Park Elementary for too much rote drill of academic skills in her classroom, and, when she carries out activities like storytelling and story acting, as she did with Daniella and the class, for not focusing enough on academics. How are teachers to reconcile the seemingly conflicting goals to teach fundamental knowledge needed for school success while creating classroom settings that motivate and inspire young children to learn? Is there an educational path toward nurturing the literate, thoughtful, well-educated, articulate children we seek in our schools that does not leave us choosing between skill mastery and meaningful learning? Lev Vygotsky and Vivian Paley offer an alternative, and my work with Mrs. Miller helps to fill in the outlines of this new direction.

Using Vygotsky and Mrs. Paley's work together makes possible a new vision of what preschool and kindergarten education can look like. I believe that if Vygotsky had had the chance to observe Mrs. Paley at work with her children, he would have pointed immediately to pretend play, storytelling, and story acting as the key activities for realizing educational goals for young children in early childhood classrooms. Until Vygotsky, no other psychologist spelled out so clearly how imagination, words, and other children matter in an individual child's learning. The words "Let's pretend..." are symbolic mediators, tools for having ideas, clarifying them, and inventing new ones. Until Vivian Paley's writings, no one had given a rendering of how learning in pretend play by an individual child could be made possible by a teacher *along with* every other child in the group. Play, storytelling, and story acting as Mrs. Paley portrays them provide a pathway to educational achievement for not only children of middle-class educated families, but—as the experience of Mrs. Miller's children at Green Park demonstrates—those who grow up in poverty and are most in need of the promise that public education can offer.

Vygotsky's Ideas about Learning

As an undergraduate in the early 1970s, I worked as a research assistant with Michael Cole, founder of the Laboratory of Comparative Human Cognition that first opened at Rockefeller University in New York before moving to its current home at the University of California, San Diego. I worked with Michael Cole and teachers at a Head Start site in Harlem. Our goal was to explore ways to organize classroom learning to expand home and community conversational proficiencies and extend them to school learning.

One of the four-year-old Head Start children told her aunt one day while walking home from school, "I a tiger at home and a mouse at school." When her aunt told the teacher this the next day, we recognized what the child meant: that she is quiet in school but lively and talkative at home. This child was articulating what William Labov (1972) was documenting with school-age children in Harlem. In school, when and if children spoke at all, it was in short, unelaborated sentences, while outside of school they engaged in more fully developed verbal interchanges, particularly with peers. What would it take for Head Start children to bring more aggressive outgoing verbal excitement and participation to their classrooms?

While studying children's patterns of conversation inside and outside of their Head Start classrooms, Michael Cole was working on translating Vygotsky's work for American audiences. One day he handed me a page he was working on.

A child's mental development is a process that is no less simple than the growth of peas or beans in a garden; and well before the fruit appears, the gardener can discern the stages that lead to the appearance

of the fruit. It would be a poor gardener who would judge the plants
under his care only on the basis of the harvest, and equally deficient
is the educator who is able to determine nothing more than what
has already happened developmentally, that is, nothing other than a
retrospective developmental summary. (From a draft manuscript for
Mind in Society in 1974)

I could not get this image of educators as gardeners out of my
mind. Skilled teaching would include being able to see the developmental history of children up to the current point in time, ana-
lyzing what is occurring in the moment *and* having an idea about
the effect of current activities in shaping the children's future. I was
drawn to the idea of standing in the present and being able to say
something about the past and future. What would it be like to be
a teacher with a class of children having a view of where they have
come from, and where they are headed?

One aspect of Vygotsky's genius was in realizing that when describing development, two levels need to be specified, not just one.
Educators and psychologists need to be watchful like the gardener
describing what has already developed, what represents fully developed cycles of change and growth. In addition, they need to describe what is in the process of formation, "the buds and flowers"
of development that anticipate the fruit to come in the harvest.
Vygotsky was the first to develop a framework for thinking about a
child's actual level of development, those parts of a child's thinking
and development that have matured, and the potential, those aspects that are in the process of unfolding.

Vygotsky went further to specify how to detect the area between
the two points of growth: the point of current mastery of skills and
knowledge, and the area of the child's newly emerging competence.
He recognized the key to pinpointing what is strong and stable in
a child and what is in the process of developing is to examine carefully what happens while the child is interacting with others. He
defined this mental space as the zone of proximal development, and
described it as "the distance between the actual developmental level
as determined by independent problem solving and the level of potential development as determined through problem solving under

adult guidance or in collaboration with more capable peers" (Vygotsky 1978, 86). Thus, any child's development is characterized by two benchmarks, one describing what a child can do on his or her own, and the other what he or she can do with help from others—adults *and* peers.

Vygotsky proposes that all intellectual learning happens twice; first it is carried out between people, and then gradually it is more internally generated and sustained by each of us as individuals. He states, "It is through others that we develop into ourselves" (1981, 161). The conversations in seminar rooms guided by Michael Cole and Sylvia Scribner and colleagues in the mid-1970s at Rockefeller University began to recognize that these principles are at work in young children's schooling as well as in their home lives. The dynamics were waiting to be discovered in all arenas of life where families, communities, schools, and businesses organize themselves to benefit from teachers, coaches, mentors, trainers, and supervisors (Cole 1996).

The idea that other people are key to the unfolding of new thinking and learning in young children seems obvious, and yet in the mid-1970s, the work of Vygotsky and his colleagues began to transform the possibilities for how this process might unfold. Like other psychologists, Vygotsky said children construct knowledge, but he emphasized that children build thinking *with* other people first. He maintained that thinking is social (involves others), historical (done over time), and cultural (following the lines of group beliefs, values, and practices). An individual's thinking and reasoning emerge from participating *in* society with family, community, and teachers and classmates in school settings. Individuals inside of groups construct patterns of personal and community thinking toward a current and future world for all involved.

Vygotsky offered for the first time a way to look at the connection between what a child does with others and how those interactions are utilized and reworked in a child's mind as he or she figures out how things work in the world—at home and in school. "Development does not proceed toward socialization," he proposes, "but toward the conversion of social relations into mental functions" (1981, 165). Vygotsky also contended that new learning comes not just from adults—a child's peers, siblings, cousins, and neighborhood friends also contribute to opening up possibilities in a child's unfolding future. The important message we can take from Vygotsky is that the pattern of interactions in the classroom matters: the conversations, arguments, debates, negotiations following tears, and the explanations. These interactions are the blueprint for the child's thinking in the future.

Vivian Paley and Zones of Proximal Development

In 1974, I left New York to pursue graduate studies at the University of Chicago. Within a few short weeks of arriving, I met and observed Vivian Paley in her kindergarten classroom at the University of Chicago Laboratory Schools. I saw children making dioramas for figures they made out of clay and painting pictures at easels lined up alongside one another on one wall, where they could look at their classmates' experiments, copy one another, and talk about what they were trying out. There were children playing checkers, taking care of babies in the doll corner, and using wooden beads as their vegetables for chicken soup. Children were building elaborate forts in the block area and watching a goldfish as it darted around the thick green grass of the fish tank.

The volume of conversation in every corner of the classroom was deafening, like nothing I had ever heard among a group of children. Rather than teachers instructing, asking questions, and children answering, the dialogue flowed among children and their teacher. I had never seen children play in school with such intensity. It was not a part of my own kindergarten experience and not part of the Head Start programs I worked with in New York. I was overwhelmed with the possibilities.

As Mrs. Paley signaled the group to gather on the rug for music and stories, I saw another side of teaching children I had never heard of or thought possible. She was trying to tame a lion, searching for the wavelength of one of the most exciting and challenging children in the class, Wally, who was shaking the ground she stood on as a teacher. A few years later, she published her account of trying to understand this child in *Wally's Stories*.

When I began to play the piano, [Wally] leaps over Lisa and Rose to get to the piano first, but before the song is finished he is on the outer edge of the rug, growling.

"Don't make that noise, Wally," I say.

"It's a warning growl."

"Not at piano time."

"I'm guarding the lions," he whispers. "The growl means I hear a suspicious noise." The children stop squirming and watch Wally as he crouches in concentration. Several boys copy his pose and give low growls. (1981, 7)

A week or two later during a visit to her classroom, I heard Mrs. Paley pick up on a comment from Wally to discuss with the children, which she also recounted in *Wally's Stories*.

One day at lunch, Wally says, "I'm going to become a mother lion when I grow up."

"A mother lion?" I ask. "Can you become a mother lion?"

"Sure. The library has everything. Even magic. When I am eight I can learn magic. That's how."

"Why a mother lion?"

"Because I would have babies and do the mommy work. They stay at home and take care of babies. Daddy lions go to work and have to walk fast."

Deana has been listening. "People can't turn into animals."

"That's true," Wally says.

"You changed your mind, Wally?" I ask.

"It *is* true, what she said. But I'm going to use magic."

"Oh, I didn't hear him say that." Deana leans forward. "If he uses magic he might. Maybe. It's very hard to do."

Fred joins in. "I might become a daddy crocodile. Every time a person tries to kill them they can swat at their guns."

"Fred," I ask, "do you believe Wally can become a mother lion?"

"No. Only if he practices very hard." (1981, 7–8)

During a third visit to her classroom, I watched Mrs. Paley read the children a storybook that they then acted out. A shy and quiet

child, Rose, took the role of a character "drinking the sea." The class
had acted out *The Carrot Seed* (Krauss 1945) a few days before, and
when Rose heard "sea," she thought of the word "seed" and pro-
ceeded to act out swallowing a seed. Her misunderstanding of this
one critical word became evident while she stood in the middle of
the rug with the whole class watching, a moment that could have
ended in embarrassment and humiliation. Wally changed everything in a second, using his fluency in pretend play to rescue Rose.
Mrs. Paley also detailed this incident in *Wally's Stories*.

> When Rose put a bead on the rug, and pretended to swallow it, the
> children asked what she was doing.
> "I'm eating the seed, that's what," she said. Eddie saw the error
> first. "No, that's for planting. This is water. You know, a sea."
> Rose was perplexed. Seeing that she had made a mistake, she
> stopped listening.
> Wally took the bead out of her hand. "Pretend a fairy changed the
> seed into a big ocean. They call that a sea and sometimes they call it an
> ocean. Now just drink it up like the man in the book. Blow up your
> cheeks like this. Then blow it out this way." Rose copied every motion
> Wally made and then did it by herself, grinning at him.
> I would not have explained the difference between "sea" and
> "seed" by magically turning a seed into a sea. Yet why not? Wally's
> magic released Rose from her fear and embarrassment. Now she
> could listen and understand. (1981, 49–50)

On a return visit, I watched Mrs. Paley lead a discussion with
the class about Wally's distressing behavior on the playground. He
had been chasing and grabbing children, and pushed one down, re-
sulting in a fight and tears. Mrs. Paley spoke to Wally and the group
about the problem.

> "This is embarrassing," I tell Wally and the whole class. "I don't know
> what else to do about you, Wally."
> "Just keep reminding him," says Lisa.
> "But I continually warn him," I tell her.
> "Remind him nicely."

"Lisa, he made you cry today."
"Keep telling Wally not to be rough," she says.
Eddie agrees. "Say to him, 'Be good, Wally, will you?'"
I turn to Wally. "Your classmates don't want you to be punished."
He smiles shyly. "That's because we're friends." (1981, 10)

Who *was* this teacher, this troublesome child, and this group of children? As Mrs. Paley sets out in *Wally's Stories*, Wally awakened the thinking of every child around him, drawing out their ideas alongside his with astonishing explanations for almost everything his teacher introduced in books, science activities, cooking, and art. He was instrumental in a critical moment of learning for Rose and was the focus of group problem-solving at another moment. I saw in Mrs. Paley's classroom how each child's learning can be everyone else's business. I saw friendships effecting the goals of school learning and the kind of learning we would want for preschool and kindergarten children now and throughout their school lives.

I knew then in 1974 that these interactions among Wally, his classmates, and his teacher were the tip of the iceberg for realizing Vygotsky's theory of zones of proximal development in the classroom. Every child was giving and receiving help in daily classroom situations where they needed to learn something. I was enrolled in the educational psychology doctoral program at the University of Chicago and quickly realized I wanted to study teaching by learning to be a teacher who understood Vygotsky and Mrs. Paley's principles of learning through interaction. I spent the next two years of graduate school completing my master of science in teaching degree while working full-time as Mrs. Paley's assistant, including the opportunity for student teaching.

While Mrs. Paley was forging ahead with her own writing about classroom teaching, Vygotsky filled my thoughts about what I saw and was beginning to practice. I was sure that if Vygotsky were sitting in Mrs. Paley's classroom, he would have found a gold mine for zones of proximal development at work in the children's play, storytelling, story acting, conversations, artwork, and math problem-solving. He would have found evidence for the kind of language use that lays the groundwork for the higher-order thinking that educators hope children will achieve. Mrs. Paley saw kindergarten as "the graduate program in fantasy play" (2004, 42). Under her guidance, the children introduced characters and plots that unfolded in sustained dialogues over days and even weeks as they examined problems from many points of view and possibility in daily play, storytelling, and story acting.

Jerome Bruner summarizes Vygotsky's view of intelligence as the capacity to make use of help from others—it is not what we already know and can produce independently that counts; it is how we use our minds in relation to others to open up new horizons (1962, viii). Western psychology has a full arsenal of tests and observation protocols delineating almost every aspect of knowledge and mental disposition, with scales or rubrics to indicate whether a child has, lacks, or hasn't yet fully mastered certain skills and proficiencies. However, until Vygotsky, educators and psychologists had not considered the mind in the process of unfolding toward a new maturity, the dynamic of learning in action.

In the late 1970s, the question for psychologists was, what might thinking look like when viewed as a social, historical, and cultural construction? What might it look like to examine the connection between what a teacher says and does with children, and the children's thinking in the future? One problem I had with Vygotsky's theory was that the gardener seems to have it easy. A gardener looks over a field of plants, spots weeds that need to be pulled, identifies where the watering system has missed, and recognizes when plants need a particular fertilizer. But how does an educator account for moving children, all of whom are at a somewhat different points in development, needing and taking different kinds of nutrients from the prepared environment in preschool and kindergarten classrooms? A teacher might be able to adjust to the learning needs of a child in a tutorial or with a small group of children, but how does a teacher like Mrs. Miller adjust to the many individuals in her class of eighteen Head Start children? The comparisons between teaching and gardening were difficult to reconcile, but Vygotsky's ideas also seemed too good to pass up.

Vygotsky examined children and development in ways that are very different from what most psychologists and educators had been focusing on for more than one hundred years. He recognized that children observe, imitate, and take up new words and actions for consideration and exploration. But he did not stop there. Vygotsky offered another startling premise for human development: that the interactions that open the way for new learning begin in pretend play. For children, there is a stepping out of what is familiar into the unknown that requires a substantial new space for thinking, experimenting, considering, and creating new possibilities. It begins with pretend, with phrases such as "What if . . ."

> Play creates a zone of proximal development of the child. In play, a child always behaves beyond his average age, above his daily behavior; in play it is as though he was a head taller than himself. As in the focus of a magnifying glass, play contains all developmental tendencies in a condensed form and is itself a major source of development. (1978, 102)

Vygotsky (like Piaget) recognized that there is a substantial qualitative shift in the course of human development that occurs around eighteen to twenty-four months of age with the emergence of symbolic representation. For the first time, the possibility arises in the human mind for an object, gesture, or person to represent someone or something else. A stick becomes a magic wand, or a train, or an ice cream cone, or a tree. A child can pretend to be a mommy, dinosaur, angel, bird, or tiger. This breakthrough in human imagination forever changes the course of a child's development and subsequent learning. The opportunity to pretend, to consider hypothetical worlds as Jerome Bruner describes, is a uniquely human achievement (1986). Vygotsky recognized the opening of children's future thinking in their uniquely human capacity to play, to try out their premises in pretend first. Mrs. Paley has given the fields of psychology and education the most detailed rendering of children's change over time as a result of their play with one another.

A Curriculum for Pretending

Vivian Paley's books portray the movement of children's thinking as they weave images from storybooks, pretend play, and conver-

sation into their school activities. The following conversation between a child and Mrs. Paley was commonplace in her classroom.

"Did you know that Peter Rabbit used to be the Runaway Bunny?"
"You think it is the same character?"
"It *is* the same. Only Peter is older."
"He does seem older. His mother isn't always looking for him now."
"That's why Peter gets into trouble too much. With Mr. McGre-
gor. I don't like that part."
"But you want me to read it."
"Yeah. I just want to hear it. Because it is in my head now. So I
wanna see how it sounds." (Paley 2004, 15)

Mrs. Paley describes the pathway as she sees it from the child's
imagination to story to book discussion:

The narrative begins early. Even before the spoken word, the pictures
in the young child's mind assume a story-like quality. How else could
the dramatic play emerge so fully formed, filling up the spaces in
other people's stories? Our books and conversations work their magic
because the children meet us more than halfway. They have already
begun feeling the emotional highs and lows of the hero and victim
and are ready to climb to the next rung of the ladder. (2004, 14–15)

Mrs. Paley's curriculum for preschool and kindergarten children
is built around conversations about ideas from the children's imaginations, and ideas generated by classroom materials, the books she
reads, and the daily activities she structures. Mrs. Paley guides children in the study of story characters, their dilemmas, and circumstances from books of all genres, and from problems the children
have with one another. Pretend play and stories are the foundations
for learning in her classroom. It is here that her thinking intersects
with Vygotsky's. Vygotsky saw that pretend play is what catapults
children toward thinking, problem solving, vocabulary development, and verbal reasoning that guide their intellectual achievement now and in subsequent schooling. In Mrs. Paley's classroom,
we see the image of the students we seek in their future.

During that first year I observed Mrs. Paley in the mid-1970s, she made one of her major discoveries in teaching: the importance of acting out children's dictated stories. I had the chance to watch this master teacher move her teaching practices, and our understanding of theory, to a new level. Mrs. Paley describes her discoveries about dramatizing children's narratives in *Wally's Stories*. Her discovery came as a surprise to herself as well as to the children—and, as often happened, with the child she worked hardest to understand and connect with: Wally.

> The first time I asked Wally if he wanted to write a story he looked surprised. "You didn't teach me how to write yet," he said.
>
> "You just *tell* me the story, Wally. I'll write the words."
>
> "What should I tell about?"
>
> "You like dinosaurs. You could tell about dinosaurs."
>
> He dictated this story.
>
> "The dinosaur smashed down the city and the people got mad and put him in jail."
>
> "Is that the end?" I asked. "Did he get out?"
>
> "He promised he would be good so they let him go home and his mother was waiting."
>
> We acted out the story immediately for one reason—I felt sorry for Wally. He had been on the time-out chair twice that day, and his sadness stayed with me. I wanted to do something nice for him, and I was sure it would please him if we acted out his story.
>
> It made Wally very happy, and a flurry of story writing began that continued and grew all year. The boys dictated as many stories as the girls, and we acted out each story the day it was written if we could.
>
> Before, we had never acted out these stories. We had dramatized every other kind of printed word—fairy tales, storybooks, poems, songs—but it had always seemed enough to just write the children's words. Obviously it was not; the words did not sufficiently represent the action, which needed to be shared. For this alone, the children would give up playtime, as it was a true extension of play. (Paley 1981, 11–12)

In developing his theory of zone of proximal development, Vygotsky probably could not have imagined such an astounding addition to the repertoire of activities that a teacher might add to the classroom curriculum. If he had been observing when Mrs. Paley came upon dramatization, and saw the effect that it had on the children's daily activity, Vygotsky would have said, "Yes! This is the cornerstone to young children's learning: dramatic play re-envisioned in written form that children listen to and study as they enact the words." In dramatization, children examine the premises of their own thinking as well as the thinking of the authors of storybooks the teacher reads to the class. Dramatization, he would argue, is a core teaching activity that expands human imaginings and possibilities exponentially—that of the individual and the group as a whole who are listening and acting.

Before we take these two experts into a Head Start classroom, how can we gauge the relevance of Vygotsky and Mrs. Paley's theories and practices in relation to current academic expectations and standards for all children? How can we be sure that nurturing children's appetites for play, storytelling, and story acting sets them on a pathway to high academic achievement? Are these activities applicable in meeting the highest standards now set for the academic achievement of all children, and specifically children in a Head Start classroom growing up in economic poverty?

Chapter 2

Acting Out Stories and the Common Core State Standards

Mrs. Miller's three- and four-year-old children sit on the edge of the rug for the day's read-aloud, "The Three Billy Goats Gruff." When she is done reading, she calls four children to the center of the rug to act out the story. The children have been eager listeners and insist on each having a turn to act it out. The only way to accommodate the class is to give four different children a chance to enact the roles of the troll and the billy goats each day. The children quickly memorize the words of this story as Mrs. Miller reads it day after day: "Once upon a time there were three billy goats and the name of all three was Gruff. They wanted to go up the hillside . . ."

When the actors are done, Mrs. Miller asks them to sit, and she says, "I have a question for you. Why do you think the troll is so mean?" Chantell immediately responds, "His mama dead." Carlos says, "Yeah, she dead." Mrs. Miller tries to overlook these responses and repeats the question: "But the troll, why is he being mean to the billy goats?" Daniella replies, "She told him to do it." Mrs. Miller now responds directly to this train of thought about a mother: "But there is no mother in the story." Anthony adds, "The father, he dead too." Lawrence adds, "They both dead."

Mrs. Miller described later how thrown she was by these comments, and her feeling that the discussion was going nowhere. She asks again: "But there is no mother and father in the story. How is the troll feeling?" Juan calls out, "Mean." José explains, "He has to fight. His mommy told him to do it." Mrs. Miller makes one last attempt: "How do the billy goats feel about the troll?" Sam asserts, "They not scared." "Yeah, the little one is," Daniella argues. Mrs. Miller says, "Daniella, you think the billy goats are scared, and, Sam, you think they are not scared. Do you think they know they are OK because there are three of them and only one mean troll?" The children holler out, "Yeah!" Mrs. Miller ends the discussion by saying, "I want to keep thinking about what you are saying about the troll and the billy goats. Right now it is time for you each to pick an activity."

Mrs. Miller admitted afterward that she was anxious to get to familiar ground in the discussion with the children. At the end of the discussion, she recognized that she resorted to a yes/no question format, an approach I urge teachers to avoid if they can as such questions invite an either/or choice between two options, a seemingly good or bad one. For today, Mrs. Miller brought closure to the discussion gracefully and guided the children to their next activities.

Mrs. Miller and I met with another Head Start teacher and two kindergarten teachers the next day as part of our ongoing professional development program to discuss their experiences with read-alouds, dramatization of stories, and open-ended discussions. Mrs. Miller was not eager to report on what she felt was a failed discussion. "The children kept saying these weird things about the mother and the father," she said, as she told the group regarding her children's comments about the troll in "The Three Billy Goats Gruff." "I don't know why everyone kept repeating 'his mother died, his father died, they both died.' Why did they get hooked on this idea? I couldn't get them off it! What am I supposed to do when the group says things that don't make sense?"

I, along with the other teachers, appreciated Mrs. Miller's dilemma. We discussed ways to manage the conversation when children say things that are seemingly off topic. Teachers suggested that maybe Mrs. Miller could remind them about what the story says, and ask them to think about the words the author gives us. One teacher commented, "Maybe they are watching too much television or other violent movies."

As I listened, I tried to imagine how I would handle the situation. Then I had a powerful memory followed by a surprising thought. I have always loved the story of "The Three Billy Goats Gruff." When we were children, my older sister, brother, and I turned any table we could find into the troll's bridge to act out this story. We relished playing the biggest billy goat confronting the troll.

Suddenly, the story had a whole new meaning to me. Mrs. Miller's children understood it beautifully—the meaning of the troll's seemingly nasty behavior. But as a classroom teacher who loved reading and acting out this story with children, and as a teacher-educator coaching others to do so, I had never thought of this before. I blurted out, "They got it! The children understand the troll!" The group turned to listen. "Look at what they are saying," I continued. "The children recognize why anyone would become so wild, mean, and threaten others: he has become an orphan! He is homeless—that's why he is living under a bridge. Of course the troll's mother is dead! And his father. And yes, his mother would tell him to stand up for himself and fight to protect himself if need be. As an orphan, the troll is protecting the last bit of territory he has left: the space under a bridge. Can you believe what your children have done for us?"

The professional development time devoted to rethinking the discussion helped us realize that the children had tapped into this story's meaning immediately. It was humbling to recognize how narrow our own thinking as teachers had been in regard to background knowledge we were prepared to bring to the discussion. We had been caught up in our individual as well as collective naïveté about possible meanings the children would bring to the narrative. Mrs. Miller's experience was a reminder that the skills involved in leading an open-ended discussion take years to cultivate, and always need fine-tuning. Guiding discussions requires a belief that there are no right or wrong answers, no "off-the-wall" responses. Discussion become possible when teachers bring a commitment to exploring meanings and interpretations of texts to the group, following every lead the children offer—considering it, and asking other children as well as colleagues to wonder about each idea and how to explain it. Teaching requires a willingness to work with groups of children daily to figure out why they think and say the things they do. The insights and connections come from listening.

As my mentor Vivian Paley coached me, such skills are best learned in daily discussion opportunities with small groups of children. During my student teaching year, Mrs. Paley arranged for me to take a group of eight or ten children for snack time and lead an open-ended discussion based on something I heard a child say during the morning activity. I remember spending the first hour of the school day listening for a topic to bring up that had no "right answer." It took weeks to stop tripping over my own thinking and grammar, and months to get the hang of this type of daily conversational routine. In Vivian Paley's appendix to *Wally's Stories*, she recognized that such discussion skills are learned; they do not simply come with the title of teacher, or necessarily with a teaching license.

After our professional development meeting, Mrs. Miller was excited about returning to her children the next day to further discuss the troll and billy goats. She told them she had been thinking about what they were saying about the troll—that he was homeless, living under a bridge, and that his mommy and daddy were dead. She asked the group if this was what they were thinking. She reported at our meeting one week later that the children's eyes lit up, and that they all began talking about the troll and his fighting. She said they acted out the story again, and that now she could see and listen to what they were thinking. The following day she asked another question: "Why does the littlest billy goat cross the bridge first?" This opened the way for discussion about relationships among the billy goat brothers.

Standards

Mrs. Miller and her colleagues are pursuing the goals of the new Common Core State Standards (National Governors Association for Best Practices and Council of Chief State School Officers 2010) that envision a school curriculum with intellectual rigor. The Head Start children's participation in the daily literature activities with Mrs. Miller are surprising and exciting because they exemplify what children are like when they are eager to listen to a story, act it out, and then discuss a question exploring the story's meaning. What are the skills a teacher needs to learn to open up and sustain such daily conversations about story characters and considering events from multiple points of view? What guides teachers in uncovering new learning and exploring ideas with children more deeply? This is what Mrs. Miller and her colleagues are studying in their ongoing professional development work.

For more than a decade, the backbone of educational reform toward high-quality teaching and learning outcomes has been the development of standards. Since the late 1990s, standards have set the bar for what teachers and educational administrators seek in daily school endeavors with children in preschool through twelfth grade. There are standards for teacher qualifications and for grade-level and school performance. As of 2012, there are national standards for student outcomes and the Common Core State Standards, which have been adopted by most states across the country to ensure a college-ready population at the end of thirteen-plus years of public-school education.

In this new wave of goal setting and planning, how can we use standards to gauge the quality of teaching and learning in classrooms? Early childhood professionals are well versed in standards for professional practice as reflected in the work of the National Association for the Education of Young Children (NAEYC) and the National Board for Professional Teaching Standards. For two decades, early childhood professionals have sought to reconcile the unique characteristics of young children with the ways in which they learn best. With its evolving definition of "developmentally appropriate practice," NAEYC has sought to guide professionals in staying mindful of the complex interwoven strands of physical, intellectual, and emotional development that characterize the first eight years of life.

Birth through age eight stands as a unit of development because there are opportunities to see continuities within and across domains of development along with the reorganization and transformation of skills and thinking during this time period. The study of early childhood across the diverse and dramatically shifting terrain of young children's skills in movement, playing, listening, speaking, and building requires recognizing transformations in the child as well as in the nature of thinking and learning itself.

Standards set ideals that we aim for. Children, however, do not always show evidence of ideals. Parenting, caregiving, and teaching are the art and science of guiding children between where they are at a moment in time in relation to our ideals. There are inevitable and necessary surges forward and then seeming setbacks in progress in the pathway forward to new achievements. How do teachers reconcile educational standards with their responsibility to guide each child toward their highest potential? How do early childhood professionals design the first steps of preschool and kindergarten so that those growing up in economic or social hardship join their peers from higher economic communities in high academic achievement?

So, how do teachers reconcile educational standards with their responsibility to guide the academic learning of each child in their classrooms? How do early childhood professionals design the first steps of preschool and kindergarten children on the ladder of school success so that they join their peers from higher economic communities on a pathway to comparable school achievement?

Learning: The Generative Kind

The learning that Vygotsky and Mrs. Paley explore is the generative kind: coming to new knowledge, skill, and insight that open up more channels of connection, interest, and motivation. Such learning does not arise solely from the accumulation of information that a child observes, or that a teacher provides for students. The child seeks it, works for it, and understands it in the long run. The learning triggers a qualitative change, a transformation in the child at moments in time, and over time. Such learning becomes possible when there are relationships among teachers and peers that make room for what is human in development—getting stuck, confused, and then, after some time and effort, surging ahead with moments of insight.

Vygotsky summarizes this perspective on learning and development as follows:

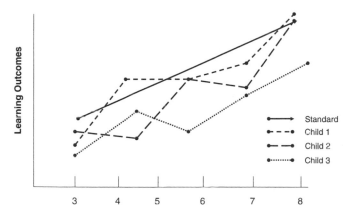

Figure 1: Learning trajectories of three children, ages three to eight

We believe that child development is a complex dialectical process characterized by periodicity, unevenness in the development of different functions, metamorphosis, or qualitative transformation from one form into another, intertwining of external and internal factors, and adaptive processes which overcome impediments the child encounters. (1978, 73)

In Mrs. Paley's classroom, teaching is about orchestrating this dialectic process for a group of children. She expects children will arrive at moments of insight at different times and in different ways during the school day and year. She also knows that children face a full range of challenges in their young lives that they can come to terms with while learning through play, discussion, and storytelling with peers and teachers. The achievements as well as the needs of one child can be recognized and appreciated by others while everyone involved comes to new places of understanding.

Figure 1 offers a way to think about the major principles at work in this view of young children's learning exemplified in Vygotsky's and Mrs. Paley's work. Imagine that we could summarize the learning profiles of three young children over a five-year period by a single score on a scale of intellectual, social, and emotional well-being. Figure 1 provides a snapshot of what we might find in three normally developing children. The profiles reveal five important principles at work.

First, standards set high expectations and goals for children's development. As parents, as a society, and as professionals, we seek a future filled with high hopes for the children who will follow us and benefit from our achievements as well as learn from our shortcomings. As figure 1 shows, standards are a step higher than reality, the most optimistic scenario for all children's potential.

Second, figure 1 shows that young children start school at different stages in their development; families have afforded their children different home and community experiences in the early months and years of life. This variability is what makes learning in school so valuable. Children thrive on and benefit from heterogeneity throughout their growing up, at home and school. They notice, imitate, and think about what is different from themselves. This is key to why other children are such an important resource in each child's learning in the classroom.

Third, children's movement toward meeting standards and expectations varies significantly. There is no "normal" child, and no single route to learning. Each child's trajectory has its own ups and downs; children venture forth, become confused, worry when their families experience hard times, and gain new resources for solving the problems they face along the way. Learning is local in that each child makes sense of and becomes master of the resources and insights offered at home and in school.

Fourth, we see that learning and growth take place over a period of years, not weeks or months that line up with the school calendar. The academic calendar is necessary for school organization and operations, but it is not a timetable designed with children's learning in mind.

Finally, the children's learning is not marked by neat linear increments in knowledge and skill. A child progresses in development but then might feel vulnerable; the child seems to slip, lose ground, and be less proficient. Bruno Bettelheim describes this developmental process as "regression as progress," in which a child takes steps backward to touch base with earlier stages of mastery and learning in order to regroup and reorganize before taking new steps forward (1982, 292). In doing so, the child gathers energy and insight, particularly when revisiting earlier learning that may not have gone well. Bettelheim describes the value of such backward steps as an opportunity to let go of current expectations in order to gain deeper understanding and an incentive to reach forward in new learning.

Pediatrician T. Berry Brazelton uses the concept of "touchpoints" to describe this same developmental path, which he notes is a basic and universal principle in human growth and development.

> The concept of "touchpoints" is a theory of the forces for change that drive a child's development. . . . Just before a surge of rapid growth in any line of development, for a short time, the child's behavior seems to fall apart. Parents can no longer rely on past accomplishments. The child often regresses in several areas and becomes difficult to understand. . . . Parents lose their own balance and become alarmed. . . . The touchpoints become a window through which parents can view the great energy that fuels the child's learning. (Brazelton and Sparrow 2006, xx)

Thus, a process of backsliding is a necessary precursor to a new surge of growth and learning.

Both Bettelheim and Brazelton provide insight into a pattern in all learning where children become confused, grow unsure, and step back into earlier stages of development. Development depends on a major reorganization and shift in how a child sees the world in order to move to a new level of thinking, feeling, and problem solving. Achievement and skills are fragile and break down while they undergo reorganization toward a more mature form. Feelings of frustration and discouragement are normal precursors to that aha moment when a child says, "Now I get it—I can do this."

Vygotsky describes the upsets and disruptions we can expect during learning.

> Steeped in the notion of evolutionary change, most workers in child psychology ignore those turning points, those spasmodic and revolutionary changes that are so frequent in the history of child devel-

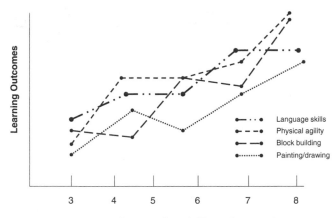

Figure 2: Development of one child, ages three to eight

opment. To the naïve mind, revolution and evolution seem incompatible and historic development continues only so long as it follows a straight line. Where upheavals occur, where the historical fabric is ruptured, the naïve mind sees only catastrophe, gaps and discontinuity. History seems to stop dead, until it once again takes the direct, linear path of development.

Scientific thought, on the contrary, sees revolution and evolution as two forms of development that are mutually related and mutually presuppose each other. Leaps in the child's development are seen by the scientific mind as no more than a moment in the general line of development. (1978, 73)

The idea that learning is the result of both revolutionary *and* evolutionary processes is what educational leaders have not been able to reconcile in current school testing and accountability practices. The problems begin here and become acute when considering the education of young children, particularly those growing up in economic hardship.

Figure 2 portrays the same profile of learning over five years—but this time by imagining that we could characterize the level of learning in different domains of an individual child's development: intellectual, social-emotional, linguistic, and physical. Here, too, are aspects of an individual that educators might focus on in a moment of time, recognizing that children's learning in the different areas of development does not move forward in a unified and smooth way. Unevenness and the need for extended periods of purposeful activities with friends are the rule rather than the exception in healthy development.

Skilled teachers like Mrs. Paley guide learning by expecting such unevenness in the various domains, recognizing the importance of a child's sometimes repetitive activities when they emerge, and protecting thinking and learning with patience and practice. She makes room for children's hunger for learning in different areas of development, and ensures that the whole class benefits from it. This is what happened when Wally helped Rose understand the word "seed."

Standards articulate goals that invite us all to reach high, but there is also the reality of striving. No child or family steps onto the road to success and achieves consistently without hitting a few speed bumps. The circuitous paths of learning must be navigated as child, as a family, and as a community. The challenge for teachers and school administrators is to expect diverse knowledge, skill, and experience among children, to expect variability in the paths to learning, and to expect development in all domains to take years, not weeks or months. Vygotsky's work urges us to see that this very diversity in a classroom and school community is what fuels the development of all children. It does not impede or hinder it.

When public-school systems gather standardized test scores on children's progress, they seek to compare, sort, and rank which children are learning, and which teachers are doing an adequate job. While there is a place for standardized testing information in examining public-school education systems, sound assessment principles call for evaluating learning using multiple tools and methods to account for outcomes. Good teaching and learning cannot be reduced to one test score; more evidence is needed, including observations on the dynamics of teaching and learning in classrooms over extended periods of time. The observations of Mrs. Miller and her students offered here provide descriptions of learning, evidence

Table 1: Students Who Are College and Career Ready in Reading, Writing, Speaking, Listening, and Language

1. They demonstrate independence.	Students can, without significant scaffolding, comprehend and evaluate complex texts across a range of types and disciplines, and they can construct effective arguments and convey intricate or multifaceted information. Likewise, students are able independently to discern a speaker's key points, request clarification, and ask relevant questions.
2. They build strong content knowledge.	Students establish a base of knowledge across a wide range of subject matter by engaging with works of quality and substance.
3. They respond to the varying demands of audience, task, purpose, and discipline.	Students . . . set and adjust purpose for reading, writing, speaking, listening, and language use as warranted by the task. They appreciate nuances, such as how the composition of an audience should affect tone when speaking and how the connotations of words affect meaning.
4. They comprehend as well as critique.	Students . . . work diligently to understand precisely what an author or speaker is saying, but they also question an author's or speaker's assumptions and premises and assess the veracity of claims and the soundness of reasoning.
5. They value evidence.	Students cite specific evidence when offering an oral or written interpretation of a text. They use relevant evidence when supporting their own points in writing and speaking, making their reasoning clear to the reader.

6. They use technology and digital media strategically and capably.	Students employ technology thoughtfully to enhance their reading, writing, speaking, listening, and language use.... They are familiar with the strengths and limitations of various technological tools and mediums and can select and use those best suited to their communication goals.
7. They come to understand other perspectives and cultures.	Students appreciate that the twenty-first-century classroom and workplace are settings in which people from often widely divergent cultures and who represent diverse experiences and perspectives must learn and work together.... Through reading great classic and contemporary works of literature representative of a variety of periods, cultures, and worldviews, students can vicariously inhabit worlds and have experiences much different than their own.

Source: *Common Core State Standards 2010.*

of teaching, and the dynamic nature of learning among young children in a classroom. The children's stories provide a more complete picture of the learning that is possible in Head Start classrooms.

The stories children tell, as well as their responses to discussion questions, also provide performance assessment data (in-the-moment verification) that Mrs. Miller's children are accountable to academic standards. The Common Core State Standards currently define the vision for educational achievement of all American children from kindergarten through twelfth grade. Table 1 presents an overview of English Language Arts (2010) outcomes.

When we listen to the Head Start children in Mrs. Miller's classroom, we hear them think carefully about the troll in "The Three Billy Goats Gruff" in ways that honor the Common Core State Standards. The children consider the author's meaning and make a surprising inference about the troll's motivation using evidence from the text, an interpretation that the teacher herself—let alone a whole group of teachers—had not yet considered. The children are already seeing multiple perspectives and, in this case, readily identify with the antagonist in a classic children's storybook. They do not waver from their point of view even when the teacher is skeptical about where their thinking is leading.

The children's responses in this discussion provide evidence of powerful thinking that is in line with goals of the Common Core State Standards. At three and four years of age in a preschool setting where they have daily practice in listening to, acting out, and discussing stories, the children demonstrate that they can think independently, gather content knowledge about people and circumstances both real and fictional, respond to the demands of a Socratic discussion format, comprehend and value evidence, and demonstrate skill in examining other people's perspectives. How did they get to this point?

We now return to Mrs. Miller's classroom on that early November day to fill out the portrait of Daniella and her classmates dictating and acting out stories with their teacher. We listen more closely to the stories at the heart of the classroom learning: those the teacher reads to the children, and those that the children dictate, both of which are acted out. What do Vygotsky and Mrs. Paley tell us about what we are seeing in the children's storytelling and acting? Along with Mrs. Miller, we observe and listen to her young children bring what they know to the construction of a place for their ideas in school and, eventually, in society as they act out one another's stories. We examine the children's activities with Mrs. Miller and her assistant, Mrs. Ortiz, keeping in mind the odds for academic achievement that the Green Park Head Start children are up against. Along with Vygotsky and Mrs. Paley, we will hold in mind the high standards for these children's educational achievement, and the professional responsibility we all have to honor the integrity of the children's development in all its complexity.

Chapter 3

"Doing Stories"

Head Start programs in many parts of the United States are half-day, three-hour programs serving three- and four-year-old children four days a week. In more rural areas, Head Start is implemented in two- or three-day sessions per week since children's bus rides to the Head Start center can take up to an hour.

The daily schedule in Mrs. Miller's Head Start classroom is tightly orchestrated to fit numerous requirements in their half-day program. In the first hour of school, the children arrive, wash their hands, and sit down for breakfast. When they finish, they clear their places, respond to their teacher's "question of the day," and then choose a book to read while waiting for everyone to gather for the first group time. The teacher leads the children in singing a welcome song, reciting a nursery rhyme, and recognizing alphabet letters. The children are then assigned to a small-group table activity while the teachers guide each group in brushing their teeth and using the washroom. As each group returns from the washroom, they resume their table activity until everyone is done.

The second part of the school day begins with a half hour of out-door time or, in bad weather, active indoor play. Then they gather for a read-aloud followed by a fifty-minute activity time, in which children can choose to build with blocks, play in the doll corner or the sand and water tables, work at the art table, play table games, make puzzles, or use the computers. The teacher and assistant circulate around the room facilitating play, completing assessments with the children, and initiating small-group activity when possible, utilizing materials in the different areas of the room.

As the playtime comes to a close, the teacher calls for cleanup time, and then gathers the children together on the rug for one last group time. They sing a final song and act out stories that were dictated. As time permits, Mrs. Miller conducts phonemic awareness activities, reading pairs of words and asking the children to identify rhymes and other units of sound. The school day ends with a snack and good-byes as family members arrive to pick up the children.

There are two teachers in each Head Start classroom with eighteen children. Mrs. Miller has a bilingual assistant, Mrs. Ortiz, because, along with African American families, this community serves Mexican families whose children are at various stages of learning English. Mrs. Ortiz more often than not takes care of serving two meals and organizes teeth-brushing and trips to the washroom; in this school, there is no bathroom adjacent to the classroom. Mrs. Ortiz is present throughout the classroom routines and activities, helping translate for the Spanish-dominant children as she can. In all facets of their work, inviting children into conversation is a priority.

Daniella, Carlos, Miguel, and their classmates began storytelling and story acting in September; it is now November. We return to their classroom to listen as the methods and tools Mrs. Paley offers are put to work: asking questions, listening, making connections in conversations while writing down stories, and, later, acting them out.

November Stories

When Daniella finishes telling her story about an angel to Mrs. Miller, several other classmates are eager to tell their own. When Daniella finishes, Maria jumps in, excited with her emerging English skills. "*Maestra*, me a story! Me a story!" she says, shaking both her hands in rapid motions as if to illustrate the words hungry to spill forth.

Maria had been playing in the doll corner next to the table where Daniella sat dictating her angel story. Mrs. Miller offers her the chair that Daniella has just vacated. Maria tells José, her best friend, to sit beside her. He is the father in their daily doll-corner play. She blurts out words in a rush of excitement while watching José's face for his reactions and monitoring Mrs. Miller's writing of each word.

> The dragon, the baby, the dad. The dragon eat the baby for lunch. The mother rescue the baby. The father trap the dragon. The baby and the mother go by the house.

Maria and José are smiling, and head off immediately to continue their story in Spanish in the doll corner.

Chantell, cooking up a storm at the doll-corner stove, says in a pushy voice to Maria, "Hey, don't touch that baby. She sleepin'. I gotta take her to the doctor. She need a shot." Mrs. Miller asks Chantell, "Do you want to tell a story about your baby that we can act out later?" Chantell says, "I got another story to tell. Maria, make sure you don't wake her. She be cryin' all night." Chantell joins Mrs. Miller at the table and launches in, pausing after each sentence while Mrs. Miller writes.

> Little Red Riding Hood was in the woods going to Grandma's house. The wolf trying to eat her up. He wants the food.

Mrs. Miller writes her final sentence and then says, "Chantell, this is almost the exact same story that you told a week ago! Listen." Mrs. Miller flips back through the pages of her notebook and finds Chantell's story from the previous week and says, "Look, here in my notebook it says 'Chantell's story.' This is from last Wednesday: 'Little Red Riding Hood and she went to her grandma. The big bad wolf is trying to eat her. He wanted the food.' You are thinking a lot about that story!" Chantell replies, "Yeah, the wolf, he not going to get it! I'm going to cook more food." She goes off to the doll corner once again.

Later, Mrs. Miller and I discuss the continuity in Chantell's narrative in story dictation. Only in these stories does her thinking about the fairy-tale characters from Mrs. Miller's read-alouds enter their conversations. She told her second story in October:

> Little Red Riding Hood. The big bad wolf comes. She go to her grandma house.

A week later she would tell the following story:

> The wolf says, "I'll huff and I'll puff and I'll blow your house down." Little Red Riding Hood said, "I'll go to my grandma's house. No, I mean my house."

Week by week, she thinks through key ideas of a classic children's story, considering the choices and decisions of the young protagonist in the face of danger.

Four-year-old Carlos is playing with three-year-old Pablo in the block area with plastic dinosaurs and zoo animals that come in small, medium, and large sizes, one and a half to five inches big. Carlos places the large dinosaurs in two lines facing each other in formation for a battle. Pablo sits silently placing the appropriate matching baby animal on the back of each larger animal. Both boys are balancing their animals with great care and precision so that the pairing of animals is exact: each large animal has its baby on its back, and there are two even rows of dinosaur warriors. Carlos is ready for the teacher to take his dictation, so as soon as she calls on him, he launches into his narrative for the emerging scene.

> The dinosaurs were playing on the grass. Then a big giant dinosaur came and scared all the dinosaurs away. And then the big dinosaur, he opens his mouth and eats all the monsters. The big monster dies.

Pablo has been staring wide-eyed at Carlos during his story. He and Carlos go back to their play while the teacher observes. She recognizes that it is almost cleanup time and is about to get up when Pablo suddenly says, "*Maestra*, mine!" He points to the animals and starts to talk excitedly in Spanish. Pablo is mostly Spanish speaking, and at this moment, the bilingual assistant is organizing toothbrushes for the daily routine following lunch. Mrs. Miller has a rudimentary knowledge of Spanish and doesn't want to miss any details in the child's dictation. She recognizes she can recruit Carlos, a fully bilingual child who has been immersed in the play episode with Pablo, to help translate. He does so readily.

Pablo dictates in a quiet and yet excited voice. He stares at Carlos as he does so. Carlos immediately translates into English as Pablo speaks, and both boys watch the piece of paper as Mrs. Miller echoes each word as she writes.

The robot carry the baby. Then they are fighting, the dragon and the baby.

The teacher rereads the two sentences in English and asks Carlos to translate them back into Spanish again for Pablo. There is a big smile on Pablo's face. Mrs. Miller asks, "Who fights, the robot and the dragon? Does the baby fight too?" Carlos consults Pablo; they exchange a few quick comments and Carlos says, "The robot fights the dragon and the baby helps the robot." Mrs. Miller replies, "Great work, boys. We will act these out in a few minutes. Carlos, thank you for helping Pablo and me write down his story." She calls for cleanup time by beginning the song that has become familiar to them all, "Clean up, clean up, everybody everywhere . . ."

I notice that Anthony, who has been building an elaborate block structure near Carlos and Pablo, stops suddenly. He looks up silently and his eyes fill with tears. He dreads the end of activity time. Anthony has the most remarkable visual artistic sensibilities of any child in the class. He points to his two-story block building with ramps and towers and says with a whimper, "My story." As a visiting teacher, I ask, "What are the words to your story?" He says, "I build a house for the cars." He watches me write each word in the notebook I carry. I look at him and say, "We have to help clean up." He nods his head ever so slightly and sadly takes the first block off his building. Children begin coming to the rug. I help Anthony dismantle his structure to make room for the group. Carlos and Pablo, with dinosaurs in their hands, push blocks toward the shelf, where other children scramble to put them on shelves.

The children gather on the rug full of excited energy. There has been sustained, focused play activity in all areas of the room. The children crawl about on the edge of the rug finding a place to sit next to friends. Mrs. Miller reminds them that it is time to settle into a spot to be ready for acting out stories.

To bring focus to the group, Mrs. Miller calls out: "Find your thumb!" She holds up her left thumb. The group is silent with all eyes on her thumb. "Get Jack ready," she says, using two fingers to mimic a boy walking. She then starts the nursery rhyme: "Jack be nimble, Jack be quick, Jack jumps over the candlestick!" She keeps her left thumb straight out in front of her and uses her right hand to model Jack "walking over" to the candlestick and then jumping over it. The children are with her. She says the rhyme again while repeating the motions as the children chant with her and their fingers jump over the candlestick. She then moves the group along to the children's narratives. She calls out, "Daniella's story is first." The girls quickly respond to the invitation to come to the center of the rug to be angels living in a castle.

When it is time for Carlos's story, he comes to the middle of the circle, directing the dinosaur actors. Mrs. Miller reminds the children of the rule: "No touching." They watch each other attentively as the big dinosaur lunges about and falls on the carpet eating monsters. The children are giddy and flopping about, all of it befitting the end of the day, a moment of fun in a shared scene about a dinosaur rumpus that Maurice Sendak, author of *Where the Wild Things Are* (1963), might have envisioned. One of the children's favorite books is a large cloth book that opens up to a desert scene with detachable felt dinosaur figures that they can act out stories with. The children are well versed in imagining dinosaur happenings from their frequent narration of the dinosaur figures.

Next is Pablo's story with a baby animal on the back of a robot, and the ensuing fight with the dragon. The boys masterfully simulate every action, and dramatizing the scene takes no more than fifteen seconds. Chantell's story follows. Mrs. Miller says to the group, "Chantell's story is about one of the stories we read a few weeks ago that she loves to think about when she dictates a story. Do you remember?" Daniella, her closest friend, shouts out: "Little Red Riding Hood!" Chantell smiles a bit sheepishly and crawls to the center of the circle. Mrs. Miller says, "Yes, so we need Little Red Riding Hood and the wolf. Chantell, which character are you going to play today?" Chantell replies, "Little Red Riding Hood." Anthony is next in line to act in the dramatizations so Mrs. Miller invites him to be the wolf. He nods, crawls to the center of the rug, and then stands up ready to act. This part needs no words. Being the wolf carries a full set of images he is ready to enact.

Each story takes no more than a minute to act out—the children know the paces of stepping on and off their stage in the center of the rug. Mrs. Miller calls Anthony back to the center of the circle for his story. She reads his single sentence while Anthony pretends to build with blocks. The children are familiar with his elaborate block structures, and many saw the one he had created on the rug just a few short minutes before. The appreciation of his story is carried in the memory of the structures he builds on that same spot. Maria's story is the grand finale. Her image is familiar, happy, and reassuring. The day ends with one of the oldest storylines: the prince killing a dragon while the mother cares for the baby. The children are ready for snack and their parents, who are about to arrive.

What have they learned in these activities of the day?

Vygotsky and Mrs. Paley Review
Learning in Head Start

One aspect of Vygotsky's theory that is particularly relevant to understanding school learning is the significance he places on learning to use words, and to do so as a tool to expand and transform what it means to understand something. For Vygotsky, the emergence of first words and their meaning is not an automatic or biological given in a developing child. Language learning is a community enterprise to communicate goals and expectations in satisfying needs, and to inform, persuade, delight, and console one another. Words used in conversations illuminate and transform the way we view experiences, and the ways we guide and direct our thinking. They are the means people of all ages use to negotiate and understand, literally and psychologically re-presenting the world to others and ourselves. Words are the opportunity to discover again the power of what we thought we already knew, or are trying to figure out. Words, and the enterprise of language learning for young children and their caregivers within family and school, shape and then transform the very nature of development itself.

As Vygotsky reminds us, words are not an accumulation of vocabulary that a child acquires and then uses. A word's meaning is the synergy of understanding between and among people. Meaning is not in the word, or in a person; it is in the relationship, in the air like a magnet pulling people together in understanding. Word meaning is general and specific, always changing and growing with use in each new situation.

Why is dramatization important and necessary to include in each school day for young children? Mrs. Paley's methods of dramatizing stories exemplify the mechanism in learning that Vygotsky envisioned as guiding development. In dramatizations of the Head Start children's stories, we watch children take their experiences and learn to put them into words. This transforms their experience into abstractions: a dramatized scene that can be examined by others, revised, and expanded on over time. When children's own narratives are dramatized alongside the narratives and stories the teacher offers to the group, the children become apprentices to every aspect of the literary enterprise: searching for words to explain images in their mind, drafting ideas, listening to and experimenting with the ideas of others, developing ideas into a logical sequence of propositions, trying them out with the group, and revising their thinking daily.

On this November day, six children, one-third of the class, have the chance to dictate stories. All eighteen children are actors in the various stories. They are learning that their own ideas, and those of others in books that are being read to them, hold new ways of thinking, feeling, and acting. This world of new ideas is coming through a process of education that is an intimate, creative, and personal enterprise for child, teacher, and the class. The children grow committed to what school has to offer because there is a dialogue between what they think and that of others around them. Children are willing partners in the educational enterprise because it becomes a dialogue among friends, not a monologue from teacher to student. It works in Mrs. Paley's classroom and in Mrs. Miller's.

In Mrs. Miller's classroom, the children's language use grows more prolific as they navigate the daily routines, talk about what they did at home before they came to school, and discuss the comings and goings of family members and what's happening around them. The children find reasons to speak that grow increasingly compelling: mealtime conversations, pretend play indoors and outdoors, storybook discussions, dictation of stories, cleanup, looking for lost items, settling disputes, and soothing hurt feelings.

In dictating stories, children learn to bring discipline to the swarm of thoughts, images, interests, and needs that crowd their minds in any moment. Anthony, who is not very talkative, finds dictating a story about his car garage some consolation in the disruptive moment of cleanup. Chantell cannot stop thinking about Little Red Riding Hood. She can bring to the group her revised drafts of the scene where the protagonist confronts the problem as often as she wants. Her classmates and teacher are happy to examine what it looks like and play it out again with its varying nuances. Children are ready to discuss and explain their choices in an unfolding narrative developing in their imaginations, and they understand the purpose and need for answering questions about who does what in a story in order to clarify stage directions.

In gathering the group on the rug, Mrs. Miller molds the class into a disciplined troupe of actors with her guided modeling of saying and acting out a nursery rhyme. In every detail of word, gesture, and conviction, she focuses the group's attention on using words. She conveys to the children that words, pretend actions, and their thinking are what matter. Their collective imagination is held in place with words. The children quickly understand key spatial reasoning words such as *over, under, on top of, here,* and *inside.* Staging stories requires matching words to mental images in a precise way that the children are invested in. The children are becoming fluent in the language of theater and story analysis: exploring characters, their motivations, how they carry out a goal, consequences, and alternative actions. The children are becoming at home in the world of school, where the currency of the realm is stories and words.

Mrs. Miller is learning new ways to engage her Head Start children in active learning bathed in conversations, debate, problem solving, and listening. She is learning to trust her children's comments in discussions of storybooks and in the scenes they bring to story dictation each day. We might go so far as to say her children's learning is natural, inevitable. However, when we step back and look at the odds of Head Start children becoming fluent and proficient in school discourse patterns, we see how much needs to be learned and how much the teacher's skill and experience in leading the classroom matter.

The activity at the core of Mrs. Miller's classroom is acting out stories: nursery rhymes, picture books, science and social studies informational books, fairy tales, and children's own dictated stories. As Mrs. Paley discovered, dramatization of the spoken and printed word is key to young children's learning to think, listen, read, and write in a deliberate, conscious way. Stories that are written down through dictation and then acted out with friends are the precursor to children doing the composing of written texts themselves and reading them. In acting out stories they have dictated, children learn to translate their story ideas into words for others to react and respond to. It is important that children are clarifying and articulating ideas *with* and *through* others, engaging in the kind of thinking and speaking that are at the heart of reading and writing with comprehension.

The work of Vivian Paley and her children, along with that of Mrs. Miller and her Head Start class, exemplify the principles that Vygotsky set out: that children build concepts about characters, events, and phenomena in the world with each other *before* and *while* they are building these understandings as individuals. Learning happens first in their relationships with one another. In scope and sequence, it is the perfect all-inclusive comprehensive curriculum *and* method of teaching that encompasses all children in learning.

As teachers learn to guide the acting out of stories—those the children dictate as well as the wealth of literature they bring to the classroom—they will understand how to channel and orchestrate the power, creativity, and motivation of the group to influence each child's learning. Teachers who use story dramatization throughout the school day are ensuring that each and every child is a part of the community committed to learning. Where did Mrs. Miller's children begin when they entered school in September? How did the children and Mrs. Miller get started?

Chapter 4

Beginnings of Storytelling
and Story Acting

It is September; the children have been in school for nine days. Mrs. Miller and Mrs. Ortiz keep the daily routines as simple as possible while the children get used to spending a few short hours away from family. I spend the morning with them exploring openings for children to tell stories and act them out. After breakfast, Mrs. Miller gathers the children on the rug for a short group time. With hands above her head and fingers wiggling, she leads the children in singing "Twinkle, Twinkle, Little Star." She then settles them for her read-aloud, "The Three Little Pigs," and invites the children to huff and puff along with her each time the wolf threatens at the door of a pig's house. When she is done, she reminds the children of the activity centers around the room and asks each child where they plan to begin: block building, water table, art area (with a hole punch for them to experiment with today), the doll corner, reading books in the library area, or tables with pattern blocks. She acknowledges each child's choice as they hurry off to different areas of the room.

I sit in a small chair next to the doll corner ready to spot a story for the first dictation. The seeds of a story will be in the emerging scenes of their pretend play. Whatever the children develop, whatever they do, can become the basis of a story to be written down and shared with the group to act out. There is a flurry of cooking, and babies who are sick that need to go to the doctor for shots. Carlos, who I have not yet heard say a word while I have been in the classroom, picks up a puppet, a parrot, and snuggles it into my lap. I ask him to tell me a story about his parrot; he takes my pen and draws elaborate squiggles. I wait as he draws his story, and then ask him what the parrot is doing. He tells me:

> When parrot gets a shot, he doesn't cry. He goes, "Caw, caw!"

Carlos lingers by me on the edge of the housekeeping area, watching two confident girls who have taken charge of the play scene.

> CHANTELL: My baby sick. We gotta take her to the doctor.
> DANIELLA: We gotta cook pizza. My baby hungry.
> CHANTELL: Hey, give me that. It hot. Here hold my baby.

Chantell thrusts her baby doll into my arms to hold while she cooks. Daniella does the same. I ask the two busy mothers to tell me the story of their babies so I can write it down for them. Chantell dictates while cooking on the stove.

> My baby likes "Twinkle, Twinkle, Little Star." She's going to get a shot. We have to pack some food for her. The baby likes hot chips.

Daniella's cooking has pots and cups falling on the floor. She too wants her story written down. She says demonstratively:

> My baby has to go to the doctor. My baby needs a shot. She will not cry.

I tell both girls that we will act out these stories when we have group time at the end of the morning. As this is the first day for dictations, they do not understand, but they continue on in their play with gusto.

A few minutes later, I pull my chair up to the block area, where boys are stacking blocks and moving plastic dinosaurs and animals in and out of scenes they set up and then crash. Again, I probe for stories. I realize play time is going to end soon, and I am determined to get dictated stories from the block area in this first day of "doing stories." I watch the boys, listen for words, and on hearing mostly sound effects accompanying their actions, I ask Pablo if I can write the words that tell us what is happening. He looks at me with a confused expression, unsure of what I am asking. I write what I see Pablo doing.

> The dinosaur eat the tiger. The dinosaur bites the tiger's head.

I ask him, "Is that your story?" He smiles and nods a big yes. I then ask José if he has a story. He stares at me with big eyes. I offer a storyline based on what I am seeing: "Can I write 'The zebra pushes the block into the truck'?" José nods his head.

Mrs. Miller watches me as I take this dictation. I recognize this might not yet look like participation on the children's part. However, it is important to jump-start this process of doing stories with narratives from two important creative sources of conversation and imagination in the classroom: the doll corner and block area. There is a third boy in the block area, Lawrence. I ask him if he has a story to tell. He describes the pile of blocks that just went spilling over.

> The pig build a house. The dinosaur knock it down. The dinosaur crash it down.

Lawrence goes on to rebuild the house with the dinosaur inside his structure this time. Within two minutes, the teachers call for cleanup time. This takes a good ten minutes; the routines of getting everything back onto shelves, its "resting place" as the teachers call it, is still new to the children.

Mrs. Miller gathers the children on the rug with music for "The Hokey Pokey" playing. She begins to clap her hands in rhythm to the song and wiggle her body. The children follow her; Mrs. Miller guides them in shaking their left foot, right foot, and onward through the song. She then asks the children to sit on the edge of the large rectangular rug; this is the setup needed to act out stories. She tells the group, "Mrs. McNamee is going to help us act out the stories some of you told today."

I hold up the spiral notebook and say to the group, "Boys and girls, while you were playing, I was watching. Some of you told a story. I wrote down your words in this notebook. Now we will act them out. Here are the stories from today. Carlos's story is the first one." I gesture for Carlos to come to the center of the rug to act out his story. I ask him, "Would you like to be the parrot?" He nods his head. I ask the boy next to him to be the doctor who gives the parrot a shot. Both boys come forward slowly. To guide them I ask, "Carlos, what does a parrot look like? How can you show us that you are a parrot?" Carlos folds his arms as if they are wings and flaps them. I prompt him, "Do the 'caw caw' sound that the parrot makes." Carlos gives a quiet, "Caw, caw." I encourage him by saying, "Good work. You have your wings and you are ready to caw!" I ask Miguel, "Show us what a doctor looks like." Mrs. Ortiz translates this into Spanish, telling Miguel to pretend to be a doctor with a needle in his hand.

I then read the story slowly, phrase by phrase, to be sure we see each word in action. I tell the group, "We are going to watch carefully as Miguel *pretends* to give the parrot a shot. He's not going to touch Carlos. Let's watch Miguel as he does this." I invite Miguel to stand about eighteen inches from Carlos and pretend to give the parrot a shot. The story is a good one to act out, very simple to follow. I compliment both boys as soon as the cawing happens, point to their seats on the edge of the rug, and announce that the first story is done; it took about twelve happy seconds. I move along to the next story. We only have six minutes for this activity before the children have snack and go home, so I keep the pace moving.

Chantell jumps up when I announce that her story is next. She is comfortable with this one-person story and acts out the motions of a busy mother holding her baby who likes hot chips. When the story opens with the baby liking "Twinkle, Twinkle, Little Star," I ask Chantell if we can all sing it to her baby. She nods and smiles. I begin singing and motion for the children to join me. The pretend baby in Chantell's arms looks peaceful.

Daniella is on her feet when I signal that her story is next. She too holds a pretend baby in her arms as I provide the brief narrative.

I call up another child to be the doctor. I coach Daniella, "Tell the doctor your baby needs a shot." I demonstrate my role of feeding the children lines to enhance the acting. Daniella repeats my words as I point to the child doctor. I follow immediately with "Good story. You can take your seats. Now, for our next one. Pablo."

Pablo is Spanish speaking with some emerging English. He stares when I call his name. I motion him to the center of the rug with a big smile accompanying my gesture. Mrs. Ortiz encourages him in Spanish, and he comes with some hesitancy. I tell the group: "Pablo was playing in the block area with José and Lawrence. They had plastic animals and dinosaurs in their block buildings." I pause as Mrs. Ortiz translates this message to Pablo and the other six children who are English-language learners. I continue, "Here are their stories. I helped them put words to what they were doing so we could act out the stories now. Watch."

Mrs. Ortiz and I are like dance partners, each of us speaking while allowing room for the other to translate simultaneously. I tell Pablo and the group that all the children will act out this story with him while watching what he does. This is an adaptation of story dramatization that I want to demonstrate early on to help potentially shy children as well as the English-language learners. I coach him, and Mrs. Ortiz translates: "Pablo, pretend you have a dinosaur in one hand and a tiger in the other. Now the dinosaur is going to eat that tiger. Let's see how you do it with your hands." Pablo and the children all have one hand pretending to bite the fingers on their other hand. They are laughing and giggling. I say, "Thank you Pablo! Now, José's story."

Pablo and José switch places. José crawls into the circle grinning. I read: "The zebra pushes the block into the truck." He stares at me, unsure of what to do. Mrs. Ortiz says in Spanish, "José, I saw you push the zebra right into the truck. Do it!" This time it is José's teacher who offers the image for dramatization. She pretends to be holding a block in both hands, and pushes it toward an imaginary truck. I have to admit, I did not have a plan of how to enact this scene, but Mrs. Ortiz was ready to help improvise in the moment. The children happily do this simple pushing motion and begin to roll on the floor like a tipped-over truck. I imagined both Mrs. Miller and Mrs. Ortiz were thinking I was guiding the group right out of control.

"The last story is Lawrence's," I call out. Lawrence crawls into the circle. I make this a one-person enactment in order to reestablish order and focus on the author. I ask Lawrence to pretend that he has blocks in front of him. I narrate, "First he is the pig building a house. Build your house, pig." Lawrence pretends to stack blocks. "Now, pretend your hand is a dinosaur. Make it look like a dinosaur's head." Lawrence does so. He has hardly said a word in school so far; now he is the star in a crashing building scene. He pretends to crash the pile of imaginary blocks and everyone claps. The teacher calls the children to wash their hands before their snack. I help dispense soap as the children wash their hands while chattering about dinosaurs, shots from a doctor, and the three pigs.

When the children go home, Mrs. Miller and I discuss what happened. The afternoon held a number of breakthroughs, including ample evidence that the children's minds are full of images they will put into words and act out when invited to, even though the initial request is awkward and unfamiliar. Their dictated stories during free playtime contain imagery derived from school experiences without any prompting from us for these references. They were thinking about the read-aloud, "The Three Little Pigs," and the nursery rhyme "Twinkle, Twinkle, Little Star," weaving threads from these narratives into their own unfolding imaginings.

Inviting the children to tell these first stories is like turning on the faucet in a sink where the water has never been turned on before. The logistics and routines for storytelling and story acting are not familiar or smooth yet. The process begins when the teacher looks for stories, and then invites and coaxes children to verbalize them. The children's images come sputtering forth and I scramble to understand them, their dialect, home language, and shyness, while capturing the words that come. Even with these rough edges, the children are eager and willing to participate as I walk them through the motions of staging their stories. Perhaps their willingness is a response to teachers' interest in what they are thinking and doing.

Story dictation and dramatization require listening, and that is a good way to nurture friendship, learning, and lots of talk about ideas.

Day Two

Ten days later, I come for my second visit on a gorgeous balmy September day. The class starts their day with the nursery rhyme "Mary Had a Little Lamb." The children recite it, sing it, and then listen for rhyming words as the teacher repeats words like *snow* and *go*. As they finish, I suggest we act out the nursery rhyme; it has a role for everyone. I am eager to jump-start the use of this most universal language among children, both mono- and bilingual. The children watch attentively.

I pick the child next to Mrs. Miller in the circle and invite her to be Mary; the next child, a boy, to be the teacher; and the next child, a girl, to be the lamb. I ask the child playing the lamb, "How can you show us that you are a lamb? What does a lamb look like?" She immediately flops down on her knees and imitates an animal on all fours. I respond, "Great!" Turning to the girl playing Mary, I say to her, "Show us that you love your little lamb!" She goes over to the child on all fours and pets her head and the lamb nuzzles up against her leg like a cat. I say, "Yes, that is exactly what Mary and her lamb look like! Now, teacher, you come stand here on the edge of the circle until Mary and the lamb come to school. We need everyone else sitting around the edge of the rug to play the part of the children who 'laugh and play to see a lamb at school.'"

I continue, "Now, the poem says the lamb's fleece was white as snow. What's fleece?" The children stare silently. They look at their teacher, who rubs her arms and says, "Remember all that wool we talked about that we get from the lamb? The fleece is all that warm woolly fur on the lamb." I add, "Let's pretend to be lambs for a minute. Feel that warm fleece, that warm woolly hair on your body." The children rub their arms and watch their teachers pretend there is a thick coat of wool on them.

I move along, saying, "Good, now we are ready to act out our poem." I tell the group, "Now say the poem with me while we watch the lamb with Mary and her teacher. 'Mary had a little lamb . . .'" I pause to coach the actors: "Mary, walk around with your little lamb following." The children start moving about the middle of the carpet. "Great! '. . . whose fleece was white as snow.' Rub her fleece, Mary!" Mary does so; she leans over to pet the lamb's back. "'And everywhere that Mary went, the lamb was sure to go.'" I pause so that we can see Mary and the lamb go around the middle of the rug once. Then we continue: "'It followed her to school one day . . .' Pretend now that you are walking to school. Walk toward your teacher. '. . . which was against the rules.' Now, teacher, show us that lambs cannot come to school." The teacher wags his finger at Mary and the lamb. I prompt him, "Teacher, tell her: No lambs in school!" Sam repeats the prompt, "No lambs in school." Mary and the lamb stop moving.

I lead the children in the last verse: "'It made the children laugh and play to see a lamb at school.' Now, everyone, pretend to laugh and play right where you are sitting on the edge of the rug as you see Mary and her lamb." The children grin and laugh. Some call out, "No lambs!" "You are in school!" The children are now giggly and ready for the next activity, a good long outdoor time that the teacher has planned for this sunny day.

The teachers guide the group in getting their coats and lining up to go outside. Once on the playground, the children are off and running in an enclosed area with a foam pad under the climbing structures. After about ten minutes of play, a child trips and falls, causing a bloody nose. The teacher gives her full attention to the injured boy and tells the children who are crowding around that the class will stay outside a little longer while she and the child sit with an ice pack on the back of his neck. When we come back to the classroom, there is time for a very short activity period. The children go to the various play areas, and I look to see if there is any interest in stories. Even with the commotion in the playground, three children are immediately at my side: first-time storytellers Charleyne and Anthony, along with Carlos, who could not wait to have another turn at this activity.

Charleyne is quiet but confident. She dictates carefully, line by line, as I write.

I like a princess.
I like Dora.
I like going to school.
I play with my friends.
I wash my hands and my grandma take me to school.
I love my mommy.

Carlos tells his own story excitedly.

The doggy ran after the girl. She find a girl. She find a lamb. They went to school.

Carlos is thinking about the nursery rhyme that his teacher read to them, taking the ideas presented earlier in the day and putting them into a story format in his own words. Carlos's dictated story and its dramatization with his classmates provide a window into the dialogue between ideas that the teacher offers in the classroom and the children's uptake. This dialogue would not be visible without the dictation process. A similar process of influence follows with Anthony's first story.

Anthony dictates a story re-creating a book about sharks that he loves to look at, and that Mrs. Miller read the day before.

Once there was a shark with a big eye. There was a sea horse who went hopping. The shark went up to the sea horse. Then a dolphin. It got the dolphin.

Anthony enacts the motions of the shark, sea horse, and dolphin with his hands as he dictates. Mrs. Miller confirmed later that he mimicked exactly how the class had accompanied her reading of this science book, creating fish images with their hands pictured on each page. His story attests to the children's attentive ear for new material in the storytelling environment. Literature, science, social studies, and math concepts enter into the children's imagination and are processed as stories that take on new meaning when acted out.

When we act out Charleyne's, Carlos's, and Anthony's stories, the children are more animated than a week ago, and many are raising their hands to have a part in the dramatization. Their eagerness to participate is noticeable. I remind the group that the author of the story can choose to play whatever role he or she wants. "For the rest of the parts, I will ask each one of you around the edge of the rug, one at a time, if you want to play the next role that comes along. If you want to play that part, you come into the center of the rug. If you don't want to play that part, you say 'No thanks.' That's how we know who plays a part as we act out the stories: we go around the circle asking people."

This process of taking on roles to act out stories goes against the practice in many classrooms in which the teacher picks children who are sitting quietly for tasks or special roles, or lets other children pick friends and classmates for a role or responsibility. As Vivian Paley discovered and wrote about in *You Can't Say You Can't Play* (1992), the teacher assigning roles to one child after another around the circle defines friendship as it must be announced in school. She also discusses this practice in the documentary *Storytelling and Story Acting with Vivian Gussin Paley* (Matlock 2002; Matlock and Testo 2001). She explains that friendship in school, and in a democratic society, is nondiscriminatory and inclusive; it is not about picking your best friends at the expense of others' interests. It is about fair and equal access to participation in all that the group is doing, and each individual developing relationships with each and every participant in the community. Thus it is the teacher who must ensure this ethic of fairness by asserting the class rule: the author of the story can choose to play a role in the dramatization of his or her story, but all other characters are offered to children sitting around the edge of the rug one after another.

When teachers guide children stepping into each other's stories in every different kind of character and plot imaginable, finding a friend in school becomes possible. The teacher offering parts to all children every day without exception demonstrates friendship that is built on acceptance, respect, and interest in what each individual child brings to the group in school. It is a good way to build a com-

munity that examines and practices the premise of friendship in a
democracy.

Charleyne's story dramatization includes herself and two other
girls who play the grandma and mommy. She is the princess who
morphs into Dora, and then the girl going to school to play with
her friends. When a story presents the opportunity for everyone to
play a part in the dramatization, I seize the moment for community-
wide participation. In this story, the class readily plays the part of
the friends Charleyne likes to be with. As I move around the circle
inviting children to take parts, two boys turn down the roles of
grandma and mommy. This story invited a strong identification of
girls with their mothers.

Charleyne's story turned out to be a magnificent ode to a good
day in school: a poem from a four-year-old naming several favorite
imaginary identities (princess, Dora), affirming her love in coming
to school to play with friends, noting the certainty of routine that
holds this new experience in place (washing hands, her grandma
taking her to school), and declaring her love for her mother. This
child's first story is a ballad right from the heart, and became a part
of the literary possibilities in this emerging community of writers.
What an exquisite achievement on this second day of storytelling!
But there were still surprises to come that day.

When we finish the three stories, Mrs. Miller moves the children
along to hand washing, snack, and then going-home time. Daniella,
who told a story on the first day, immediately cries out, "But I didn't
get to tell my story!" She panics at the thought that she will not get
a turn. The teacher tries to comfort her, but she won't have it. I am
curious about what story she might tell, and also hope she does not
have to leave school with such disappointment, knowing that she
might have to wait a week. I tell her to wash her hands, go to the
snack table, and I will come write her story down while she eats. I
know if she dictates even two sentences, we can act them out in under a minute. Daniella dashes off to wash her hands, and I join her
at the snack table. Her story comes without a moment's hesitancy.

A monster was chasing the little girl in her closet. He run and grab the
little girl and snatched her and ate her.

The teacher read Mercer Mayer's *There's a Nightmare in My Closet* that day for the read-aloud, and the thrill of a monster chasing a little girl was yearning to be played out.

I tell Daniella we will go right to the rug, where several children are waiting for family members to arrive to take them home. I move quickly to get this enactment in before Daniella has to leave. Daniella cannot wait to be the little girl. I ask the first child I see, Lawrence, if he would like to be the monster. Lawrence is a physically small boy who rarely says a word and is often in a dream world of his own, not always tuned in with what is happening around him. In many ways, he seems like the least likely child to act alongside Daniella, now the most outgoing thespian in the class.

I ask, "Lawrence, will you be a monster in Daniella's story?" He seems a bit confused by what I am asking—this is not the setting where I had initiated such activity before—but he nods and starts to smile. I tell him, "Pretend to chase Daniella around the rug, and then to pretend to grab her and eat her." I emphasize *pretend.* Crouching beside both children amid the others leaving for home, I demonstrate how to pretend grab and pretend eat Daniella without touching her. Daniella loves this experience and giggles with happiness as Lawrence pretends to eat her up. The whole production from dictation through to dramatization takes maybe three and a half minutes. Daniella leaves for home with her grandma, a big smile, and a sense that the school day is complete.

Day Three

My next visit came one week later. The children are sitting at breakfast when I pull up a chair to listen to their conversations. From across the table, Daniella says to me in a slow yet clear voice, "You know, last night I was thinking 'bout that play I wrote last time. Can we act it out today?" I am stunned with shock and excitement that she was thinking of her story from one week ago. What made it possible for this child to express her wish to act out her story of seven days ago so clearly? And how is it possible that she already thinks of herself as a playwright?

I tell Daniella, "I was also thinking about how rushed we were at the end of the day last time I was here, and that your story was such a good one to act out. Yes, let's act it out again when the group is together. We will ask Lawrence to play the part of the monster again." I open my notebook and reread her story to her. Her face lights up; her memory of the story was re-created in dazzling clarity now through the written word. She is becoming hooked on the power and purpose of written language.

I have several goals in mind for this third day of our story writing and acting:

1. To teach the concept of acting with no touching; Daniella's story of the monster grabbing her and eating her up is the perfect opportunity to demonstrate how actors do this.
2. To demonstrate how we pick actors for dramatization—going around the circle asking each child if they would like to play the part that needs an actor. Even so, they still revert to shouting "Me, me" when they hear a character called out for a story.
3. To reach out to more of the Spanish-speaking children to ensure their participation in the activity, with Mrs. Ortiz helping to translate when possible.

The teacher gathers the children on the rug for their beginning-of-the-day activities. Mrs. Miller happily lets me add the dramatization of Daniella's story to the group time to reinforce the connection she is making between last week and today. I tell the children: "Last week, Daniella told a story right at the end of the afternoon, and Lawrence helped her act it out. Today we will act it out so that you can all see it." The children eagerly raise their hands, and one calls out, "I want to do a story!" I tell the group that I will write down their stories during activity time, but right now we will act out Daniella's story since we didn't get to last week. I tell the children, "Watch how Lawrence pretends to be a monster that grabs the little girl in the story and eats her. Watch how he does this. Notice that he is not going to ever touch her. He just pretends."

As a warm-up, and to more fully demonstrate the concept of pretending in story acting, I invite all of the children to act. "Pretend we are all monsters. Show me what a scary monster looks like." We all hold up our hands with fingers curved into claws. I coach them, "Pretend you are eating the little girl." The children make grabbing motions in the air as we pretend to eat the little girl. Daniella laughs out loud as the whole group does this.

Lawrence silently watches the children around him. Last week, Lawrence went along with what this "big kid" asked of him without saying a word. Today when I call Lawrence into the circle with Daniella, he is more than a head taller in his garden of growth, smiling, on top of the world. This little boy who barely says a word to anyone is now a star in Daniella's story. We act out the story twice with Daniella and Lawrence, and then with two other children sitting next to Lawrence. The story sets the pace for those that follow that day.

The children sit while their teacher rereads "The Three Little Pigs" with great animation. She invites children into the circle to act out scenes from the story as she goes. The children are quick studies for this way of participating in exploring the meaning of words.

Having made progress in demonstrating the story-acting routines, my next goal is to reach out to more Spanish-speaking children, most of whom are boys, and find a way to bridge languages in storytelling and story acting. I go to the art table to see Demetrius and Anthony coloring pictures. Demetrius is coloring a ghost holding a trick-or-treat bag. Demetrius speaks in a low voice. I cannot hear him so I ask him to repeat it. I look around to see if I can spot Mrs. Ortiz to translate. Then I hear English words: the brother and the ghost. I quickly say back to him, "The brother and the ghost?" He nods. I scribble this down as fast as I can, repeating every word as I write. He points to the trick-or-treat bag and says: "box." Anthony adds: "He had a box." I repeat this as I write. Then I hear Demetrius say, "He hold it." I write this down. He is finished.

The brother and the ghost. He had a box. He hold it.

Demetrius puts his crayon away and picks up his paper to bring to his cubby. I tell him, "We will act this out with the group."

I realized later I could have acted out Demetrius's story right there on the spot with Anthony so that he could see his story immediately. I could see how tentative his understanding was about what we were doing while sitting on the rug acting out stories as a class. I realized the growing impact that dramatization could have helping the child connect the various representations of his thinking that were unfolding: his drawing, dictation, and the enactment of it. One of the adaptations in the dictation methods I made during the rest of the year was acting out stories right after dictation when possible. In this case, enacting the story would also have strengthened the connection between Anthony and Demetrius learning to help each other listen to and tell stories.

I follow Anthony to the block area and watch him build with blocks. I ask him to tell me the story so we could act it out. Anthony dictates:

> I build a strong house. The wolf cannot blow it. The pig says, "I went in my house."

He is pleased with this. Mrs. Ortiz calls out that it is almost time for cleanup. I look for Daniella because I am learning that she longs to tell a story. She is in the house area and comes promptly.

> The little girl and her grandma was going to her auntie's house. They saw a scary thing. It was a parrot. She was really scared. It was not nice at all. The parrot slapped the little girl. Then he flied away.

Daniella says she wants to be the little girl. Carlos, the other confident storyteller, is right by her with the parrot puppet. I am astounded that the lead character in the first story told in this classroom by Carlos is what comes to Daniella's mind in the urgency of the moment on this third day of the activity. These two friends standing side by side are thinking about ideas they now have in common while moving their own thinking forward.

Carlos then has to tell his own story. He pushes right in to make sure I keep writing.

The monster was climbing up the wall. The girl saw the monster. She turned into a monster and tried to follow the monster. Then the monkey came and was the girl's friend. She catched the monkey.

Carlos says he wants to be the monkey. Then he thinks of more that he wants in his story. A lot more. We have time for one more sentence.

Then Batman come and hit the little girl because the monkey was Batman's friend.

At the group time before snack, we act out these stories. I call the first child to the center of the rug, "Come, Demetrius, we will act out your story." Mrs. Ortiz is on the edge of the circle translating simultaneously as we go. Demetrius looks confused and startled. He freezes. I ask him: "Do you want to act out your story?" Mrs. Ortiz and I are in synchrony with our coaxing of him in two languages. Demetrius is silent, unresponsive. I look at him across the circle; his eyes are glued to mine. Other children are eagerly volunteering to play the parts. I ask them to wait while I check with Demetrius about what he wants.

I ask him again; Mrs. Ortiz follows up. I tell him, "Listen to your story. See if you want to act it out." I read his story, pausing after each sentence while Mrs. Ortiz brings his words to the group in Spanish. Mrs. Ortiz says "ghost" several times in Spanish with a question mark checking to see if he remembers the ghost he talked about. I wait, holding the group in this moment of suspended silence. I want Demetrius to see and hear his story, to know that we are acting out *his* story. Perhaps I should have acted out someone else's story first?

All of a sudden, his eyes light up. The words and this request have found a meaning. He scrambles into the middle of the circle. I say, "Demetrius is the ghost." Mrs. Ortiz translates, and I call the boy next to him to be the brother. He is there in an instant. I read the first sentence; Mrs. Ortiz follows. The boys wave their arms like ghosts. I read the next line; the teacher translates. The boys both pretend to have a box. They act out holding it tight. They are both pleased and grinning.

We go on to act out the next three stories. I emphasize pretending actions in each one. The children have got it: the wolf trying to blow a house down, the parrot slapping the little girl, and Batman doing so as well. The children are eager and ready for acting. They go for their snack and greet parents who are starting to arrive.

On this third day of "doing stories," five weeks into the school year, Mrs. Miller, Mrs. Ortiz, and I recognize a new set of achievements for these children. First, Carlos and Daniella are emerging as leaders in their class in storytelling and story acting. They see themselves as playwrights, and they seek out, even demand, time to dictate a story. Second, Lawrence, once one of the most silent members of the class, has now been a willing lead actor in Daniella's ghost story. Third, Demetrius and José, two English-language learners, have made their breakthrough into the storytelling community with their narratives taking the limelight with the help of the teacher's translations. Mrs. Miller and Mrs. Ortiz are ready to keep the notebook for taking children's dictated stories that are acted out.

Teaching and Learning in Storytelling and Story Acting

The children's achievements in the initial three morning sessions introducing storytelling and acting were remarkable, and the intricacies of their narratives only grew more exciting each week. The demands on verbal skills that the storytelling and story-acting activities afford are visible in any individual child's story, but take on a new significance when viewed in relation to the group's thinking and the teacher's facilitation of it. Vivian Paley's writings present portraits of children who are articulate, inventive thinkers, and generous citizens in the community. She has maintained that the ability to think, reason, converse, debate, and create are the human potential of all children that can be realized when a teacher is prepared to listen and ask questions. She shows us that techniques for uncovering children's language and literary future, using children's literature, paper, pencil, and careful listening and speaking, are teaching tools we can well afford to invest in.

In studying the storytelling and story-acting curricular practices in Mrs. Miller's classroom, we have the chance to see their benefits at work in a way that might not otherwise be apparent. With Lev Vygotsky's commentary, we gain more insight as to why these activities are essential, especially for children who may not come to school primed with experience in conversing with others. Seven reasons why these activities are powerful, important, and effective emerge on close examination.

1. Storytelling and story acting are a socially equalizing curriculum. The children in Mrs. Miller's classroom are very much the peers of the children Mrs. Paley has described for decades in her own classrooms and those across America where she has visited. Children attending public school in an impoverished neighborhood are poised to join their peers of all income, racial, and language backgrounds as articulate, imaginative, creative thinkers who learn from listening to and helping others.

Mrs. Paley is a teacher who understands how to create the conditions that open the way for children's potential in speaking, thinking about, and composing their own stories with her as well as with their peers in the classroom. As the work in Mrs. Miller and Mrs. Ortiz's classroom demonstrates, the process of activating a preschool child's potential begins with seeding the ground with conversation and stories that the teacher reads and tells while listening to those the children have to tell.

Classrooms led by teachers like Mrs. Paley and Mrs. Miller align paper and pencil with activity centers—a library, blocks, miniature animals and people, a doll corner, a Play-Doh table, puzzles and pattern blocks, and small objects like buttons for counting, sorting, and comparing. The seeds of writing emerge from materials of self-expression that include paints, colored pencils, markers, crayons, scissors, glue, a stapler, a hole punch, stencils, an alphabet display, and paper of all sizes and colors. Classrooms for rich and poor have these materials. What differs is the assumptions about the kind of interactions children from neighborhoods in economic poverty need with the teacher to jump-start their thinking and conversing in school. Mrs. Paley's curriculum supported by Vygotsky's analysis advocates for both poor and economically advantaged children to have the same exposure to and involvement in developing ideas daily in such activities in their classrooms.

2. *Storytelling and story acting illustrate how thinking emerges first among people.* Dramatization of the children's stories, as well as those the teachers read, makes it possible for children to step into a character in a scene, borrow snippets of ideas to try on for themselves, and to expand their thinking in new ways. This, Vygotsky would say, is the instantiation of the theory of thought developing among and between people first that fosters individual achievement later.

In dramatization, we see children listening to and gathering ideas from one another as well as from what the teacher offers in the stories and poems she reads to them. The children's participation in these activities stands in contrast to the heavy emphasis on recitation of the months of the year, colors of placards, and shapes in basic skills curricula that often fill the Head Start school day. In contrast, story dictation and dramatization activities privilege words: stories develop in play and conversations, are composed into written narratives with their conventions and vocal intonation, and are then reenacted at a later point in time from the printed page. Children dictating and acting out stories are immersed in learning opportunities with peers that capitalize on the active, social, and verbal nature of young children's learning.

3. *Storytelling and story acting are an inclusive curriculum.* Mrs. Paley describes the beginning of the storytelling and story-acting curriculum from an impromptu invention that emerged as an alternative to punishing a challenging child: Wally (1980). She continued to focus on the dramatization part of the activity when she found that boys would stop running around and choose to come sit at a table and seek out her time (and pen) to take down their stories *if* they were acted out. The stories from Mrs. Paley's and Mrs. Miller's students demonstrate that this activity holds meaning for all children: the shy, loud, aggressive, withdrawn, and the English-language learners.

4. Storytelling and story acting are a curriculum in word meaning. Had Vygotsky read Mrs. Paley's writings and observed Mrs. Miller's classroom, he would now say that we need to keep a close eye on dramatization. This is not a frill in the classroom curriculum, and not an arts-integration experience to include on Fridays or special occasions because it is fun and enjoyable. Vygotsky would say dramatization is a necessary experience in school for young children to get inside of word meanings in a physical and verbal way in order to understand what teachers and peers are trying to say to one another. Leading the dramatization of stories is the moment when a teacher stands at the intersection between a child's current developmental achievements and his or her future. The individual and the group are integrally related; the achievements of the group are available to each individual, and each child can benefit from as well as contribute to others.

5. Storytelling and story acting provide an entrée to the imagination, and harness its potential for school learning. Leading dramatizations is a place of privilege for teachers. Without Vygotsky, I could not have realized what such a moment in teaching young children might look like. Dramatization contains the ingredients of a child's zone of proximal development at work in an optimal way: a child interacting with others using words and actions to carefully examine the logic and premises of ideas from imaginary and hypothetical worlds as well as ideas grounding the realities around them. This is what school hopes for children: that they learn to use words to read and write fiction and informational texts in order to understand and become excited about possibilities they never thought about before. From the children's point of view, dramatization means ideas: enacting scenes and problems from literature, the sciences, math, and social studies as well as the children's stories integrating these disciplines.

6. Storytelling and story acting focus attention on the teaching skills needed to promote verbal expression and fluency. As I continued to visit Mrs. Miller's classroom, I viewed acting out the simplest of story or nursery rhyme with the children as an exciting and challenging teaching experience. Dramatization is the time of day when the teacher can see the children's thinking in the air among them all, inviting one another in opening up new possibilities in word meaning and ideas. The teacher is guiding the group in a highly structured, disciplined approach to examining the logic and premises of an idea for the benefit of each individual as well as the group, simultaneously. When participating in dramatizations, the teacher's guidance and questions stretch the children's intellectual muscle and imagination, and other children's thinking does so as well. Thinking is there on the stage with possibilities externalized.

Dramatization invites a more complete and complex view of children and their learning. Teaching is not always a nice, orderly interaction, with a teacher asking questions and children giving correct answers, as I thought over thirty-five years ago when I began studying to become a teacher. During dramatizations, children can get antsy, crawl around, and become excited about being monsters and squabbling kitty cats, and even hit another by mistake. Small daily impromptu dramatizations do not initially look grand and profound, but it is the children's experiences over time that reveal the goals and expectations we hold for children. Mrs. Paley's and Mrs. Miller's children are not learning to lock their knowledge away in a test score. In storytelling and story acting, they are appropriating knowledge and building their understanding of literature, math concepts, language, and friendship. They do this complex work of thinking and learning with one another in a rich activity, not in individual discrete skill-building exercises.

These vignettes of Head Start children emphasize what children who grow up in neighborhoods of economic poverty are learning from their teachers as well as one another. While school has always organized learning for groups of children with a teacher, educators tend to emphasize the primacy of the teacher in each child's learning. We tend to talk of children's learning as the product of a dyadic relationship: what the teacher has taught the child. However, in the profile of teaching explored here, the equation of learning is more complex. Other children matter; they are an essential part of each child's learning in school. The teacher's role is to organize interactions so that the class as a collective provides the strength and resources for each child in the group to achieve his or her potential every day in school. In a Vygotskian image of teaching and learning, every child is directly included in learning and success.

7. *Storytelling and story acting address social and emotional learning goals, promoting friendship, collaboration, and respect.* By examining children's participation in storytelling and story acting, we see that teachers are at their best when they make each child's learning everyone else's business. The relationships emerging among the children play an integral part in the learning. A teacher who provides time for children to interact and play, and who offers them a chance to insert their own ideas into a story the group can act out, offers young children an entrée into classroom life that is respectful of each child's contribution. Children grow more interested and excited to learn together how the larger community outside of home works. Preschool is the child's first step into society. Mrs. Paley and Mrs. Miller offer a portrait of a society that is vibrant with ideas, and one that prizes the spoken and written word. Lawrence steps into school and society when he acts in Daniella's story. Demetrius does so when his ghost story is acted out in Spanish and English, his quiet voice taking center stage within the group.

No teacher can give a child a friend, but activities like dramatization of children's stories and "The Three Little Pigs" set the stage for school friendships to emerge and thrive. Such friendships are a blueprint for the ways of interacting and collaborating around building ideas that we hope for future citizens in society at large. In such communities, everyone is interested in the ideas being offered, and everyone has a story to tell. "Pick me; pick me to play that part" is overruled by systematically inviting each child to consider herself or himself as the next character in any story being acted out, and as an author every day of the school year.

Children gravitate toward dramatization as it provides opportunities for learning the way their peers do it best. Teachers are not providing didactic and pedantic lessons with threats and punishment. They are mobilizing children toward friendships that invoke empathy, companionship, and borrowing of imagery in ways that shine light on new possibilities.

We have come to the cornerstones for young children's verbal
fluency in the classroom: listening to and dramatizing stories daily
while learning to be friends. How do the daily practices in Mrs.
Miller's classroom create a pathway that leads to the mastery of
reading and writing? Where are the elements of the zone of proximal development at work in these teaching practices over time—
and are they nurturing the intellectual potential of these young
children growing up in harsh economic circumstances?

Chapter 5

Changes in Development

In the Vygotskian view, the beginnings of literacy are grounded in play, the capacity to wonder, pretend, imagine, and consider possibilities. Play is essential for others to be able to enter into a dialogue with a child about new possibilities. When a teacher initiates verbal play such as singing a song or nursery rhyme, the children are engaged in an activity saturated with meaning from family and community literary history. Such activity offers children nuggets from their literary past to serve as stepping-stones to the future, inviting them to make something new using words in some yet unknown ways. When the teacher makes room for other children to influence and shape the development of each child during daily play, story dictation, and story acting, learning in school is at work.

To see how Mrs. Miller's children are gaining momentum in verbal fluency by acting out their own imaginary narratives and those drawn from children's literature, both fiction and nonfiction, we visit their classroom in March of the school year. We observe how dramatization of ideas in pretend play and story acting activates what Vygotsky sees as a dialogue between evolution and revolution in children's development and, in particular, as children step from oral into written language. The steps toward this transition come from the initiative of an attentive teacher introducing and then inviting children to participate in storytelling and story acting.

Batman and His Dad

On a sunny day in March, seventeen children arrive in Mrs. Miller's classroom. Carlos and Miguel finish breakfast and go to the rug area to read books. Miguel says he needs to use the washroom; Carlos offers to go with him. I signal to Mrs. Miller that I will go with both of them while the rest of the class is finishing breakfast. The two boys skip down the hall ahead of me. I have my notebook with me ready to take down the children's stories when a free moment presents itself; waiting with Carlos in the hallway for Miguel to use the washroom is such a moment.

Carlos has become the lead boy storyteller since the early September day when he held a puppet and told the first story in this class. He dictates a story almost every day I visit, as well as with Mrs. Miller or Mrs. Ortiz. He readily translates for the Spanish-speaking children when they want to dictate a story and Mrs. Ortiz is not available. Carlos is fully versed in the imagery of his friends and can often help clarify an idea or action that someone is trying to articulate. His favorite characters are Batman and Robin. Today, his story and its title come with ease. He knows the routine and dictates in perfect rhythm to the speed of my writing.

Batman and Robin

Batman went in his car and Robin went in Batman's car. They went together. They drive to Joker. And they fight with him. They escape. Then what happened, an explosion happened in the car. Batman and Robin are OK because they hit the cat. The cat was the bad guy. Batman sticks his arm out straight and then they happened on the explosion.

Miguel returns from the washroom and listens intently as Carlos is describing the first explosion. When Carlos is done, I say to Miguel, "Do you have a story today?" Miguel looks at me intently, silent for a moment or two. I ask him again, "Do you want to tell a story? Do you have a Batman story?" Carlos intervenes by pointing to the notebook and says, "Miguel's story can be right there. He can be Batman flying too." I ask Miguel if he wants that. He nods. I ask Miguel, "Do you want me to write 'Batman flies'?" Miguel nods again. Pointing to the whole notebook page again, Carlos says, "This whole thing is Miguel's story." Carlos generously lets Miguel be in his story and allows his story to be Miguel's too. He is willing to consider Miguel's story as an extension of his own, or even be the same one. This is the quality of a more experienced and skilled peer who can engage and encourage a newcomer to these activities.

Carlos extends his authorship to Miguel as part of sharing this time together in the hallway. Dictation is an unusual and unexpected kind of interaction inside and outside the classroom. Generally, teachers and adults don't take this kind of time for active listening to children's thinking. And yet Carlos and Daniella, born storytellers, offer their ideas readily to all who will listen in play, and now in story dictation.

In this brief hallway scene, with teachers and children passing by, I hold on to the possibility that Miguel will take a chance at putting an image into words. He has done so only once before in this school year. Tentative but eager, Miguel tells the following story, his very first, while Carlos listens.

Batman can fly. Batman flies with the guy who was his dad. And then Batman fights with the king. Batman flies with all his friends.

I can hear Mrs. Ortiz calling the children in the classroom for group time on the rug. I tell the boys that we have to go. Miguel runs to the classroom smiling. A growing friendship is shaping the start of this school day. The boys have kept each other company walking past two classrooms, and they have had my companionship and ear for listening to their stories every step of the way. My goal is to maximize the ways in which children can connect in conversation as they discover what each other thinks, and how their thinking can enrich the repertoire of ideas generated by the group and each individual within it.

Carlos and Miguel, both age four, have breakfast together, play outdoors, participate in small-group activities with their teachers, listen to read-alouds, sing songs, and, at the end of the day, listen to and act out the stories they each dictate—all while connecting their interests to that of their peers and teacher. Within this community of friends who listen and speak to one another, teachers can play a role in orchestrating the foundation for current and future schooling in oral and written language. How is the kind of transformative learning from oral to written language that Vygotsky describes, and that Mrs. Paley demonstrates, evident in Mrs. Miller's Head Start classroom? What evidence can teachers observe and gather in assessing this progress?

Explaining Change

Between the ages of three and eight, young children's proficiency in oral language rapidly expands to include reading and writing in their communicative resources. In examining the development of children learning to read and write, we see that it is not just an accumulation of alphabet, phonics, and penmanship skills that mark this growth toward literacy. The preschool and kindergarten years bring a set of new realizations about symbols. As toddlers, very young children begin to realize everything has a name, and that we can ask questions about names, places, and people, as well as make commands and statements about them. Very quickly on the heels of this realization, children discover that we can make marks on paper to represent the ideas in our heads—the pictures or the words. The transformations in how children can interact with the world are under way, propelling them toward reading and writing in a way that will change how they think and learn. By ages six and seven, children are intrigued with the rules and codes of written language. They are ready to master the conventions that give them greater command over a system they can use and benefit from in their learning. All of this unfolds in a few short years, and how they traverse these years makes a difference.

Vygotsky's work revolutionized the study of a child's development, starting with the premise that there is no such thing as a child per se, or thinking, or skills. Rather, there are particular situations with specific resources that family, community, and the activity itself afford the child. Children's development is always situated in activities; they are continuously changing and being changed by experiences and situations around them.

Vygotsky's colleagues and students, primarily Aleksei Leont'ev, recognized that children do not grow up generally or generically; they grow up in relation to specific cultural practices that involve people, their intentions and goals, and their actions and tools for accomplishing tasks. Whereas most developmental explanations attempt to describe change in children as if they were singular autonomous units of life, Vygotsky and his colleagues emphasized the necessity of studying the particulars of the situations and interactions with others that contribute to the child's learning over the course of growing up.

In a Vygotskian perspective, children learn to read and write in the context of daily activities with teachers in school settings, participating in what Peg Griffin and Michael Cole call "basic activities" (1986, 127) that call upon basic skills to carry out the activity. Children become skilled through their motivation to participate and become more competent in activities they care about. Gradually, children become more conscious and aware of the skills involved and seek opportunities to practice them. The story dictation and dramatization in Mrs. Paley's and Mrs. Miller's classrooms provide examples of basic language and literacy activities in school that children aged two and a half to three years and older can benefit from. Children are drawn to the practice of envisioning a pretend scene that they narrate to someone who records it so that others can act it out later. When carried out in school, these activities have the power to ignite and sustain literacy learning in young children from any and all economic, cultural, and language backgrounds while introducing them to the basic skills in reading and writing.

Learning in basic activities reflects a number of counterintuitive operating principles about children's learning. How can children read and write before they have learned to do so, and, in particular, before someone has taught them? Learning to read and write develops in concert with all the various verbal, mental, family, social, and emotionally important activities that children are a part of when preschool and kindergarten become settings infused with basic activities. Basic literacy activities such as reading aloud to young children, as well as acting out storybooks and the stories the children dictate, invite and nurture the stories and conversational skills. As the work of Mrs. Paley and Mrs. Miller demonstrates, conversation and stories can become staples of what children expect at school. Children gain ground quickly in the activities that tap into and invite their imagination and verbal proficiencies.

When classroom life begins with a commitment to the expression of ideas through language, the fabric for long-term, engaging school learning is woven. With children as young as two and a half to three years of age, daily exposure to phrases such as "Once upon a time" in the reading of classic storybooks provides children with a foundation in their cultural heritage through the medium of language central to literacy. Questions like "Why is the troll so mean to the billy goats?" encourage children to talk about and find meaning in stories they hear, to consider new imaginary scenarios to play out with peers, and to connect stories to personal experiences as well as classroom events. It is their classmates' and teachers' interest in what each member of the group is thinking about a new story that jump-starts children into literacy development—while holding hands figuratively and physically with new friends. Once they taste the power of ideas that flow from and contribute to the recording of stories, there is no keeping the alphabet away from them. Speaking, listening, and acting pave the way for reading and writing.

A Literary Community at Work

The day that began with Carlos's and Miguel's Batman stories was a day that called for the full concentration of all three teachers in the room. The issues in children's lives pressed through to the surface as we navigated the daily routines. At this point in the school year, Mrs. Miller and Mrs. Ortiz were happy to let me take down children's stories and lead their dramatization so I could continue to study what we were learning.

A week earlier, Charleyne dictated a story right before leaving for home. Her request was urgent, so I agreed to take down her story while reminding her that we would act it out next time I visited. As it turned out, I was glad there was no time to act it out. She described a dark and scary scene.

> The monster killed the woman. The daughter start crying. And the baby cried, "Mommy, mommy!" The mommy was dead. Now the grandfather went into the house an' said, "Where's my daughter?" He saw her and he start crying. "Oh my goodness, my daughter's dead!" He start crying.

Mrs. Miller, Mrs. Ortiz, and the children know Charleyne to be one of the happiest students in the classroom. She always has a big smile, a bubbly personality, and kind words for everyone. She gets along well with others and will join anyone in an activity, providing good company. And yet she can imagine terror and sadness. When her mother came, Charleyne told her, "I told a story!" She put on her coat and took up her backpack. Had the dictation made it possible for her to let go of the frightening image so that she could keep going in her day?

Even if there had been time, I would not have brought it to the group. I would have told Charleyne, "Your story is really scary. I'm glad you told it to me. We won't act this out because it will upset other children too." On another occasion, Mrs. Miller conveyed the same message to a child when her dictated story recounted an angry scene between her parents. In that situation, the teachers offered to join the child in one of her favorite activities, like painting or making a crown with pipe cleaners, an activity equivalent to drinking hot chocolate to bring comfort and companionship.

The following week, I wonder what Charleyne will be thinking. I am not going to revisit the story she had told, but I am curious about what her next story might be. After Mrs. Miller finished the read-aloud, as Charleyne is walking from the rug toward the shelves to pick an activity, I ask her, "Do you want to tell a story today?" She nods yes. I suggest, "Do you want to do an activity for a while, or do a story now?" Her eyes light up, she pulls out a chair, sits down, and begins to dictate without faltering, picking up on

themes that were in last week's narrative. I wonder what it means
that she carried such a line of thought with her given the huge number of events, interactions, and daily routines that had transpired
over the last seven days. But there are also important new additions.
Charleyne speaks in a steady calm voice timed to the speed of
my printing.

> The mommy carry her baby. Her dad walked in the door and
> walked in her room. He lookin' for his daughter. He liked to eat
> treats. Then he liked the numbers like 1, 2, 3, 4, 5, 6, 7, 8, 9, 10, 11, 12,
> 13, 14. He liked movies, he watch movies and he liked to do his hair.
> When the girls walked in, he said, "Why you come in and how are
> you?" He liked the girl and all her friends come in. The girls said, "Get
> out of my house! I don't like you!" And the father killed her and then
> her come back to life and she turn into a princess. And then she cut
> her father off with a knife. Then he turned into a prince. And then he
> went to work. And he

> Clap, clap, clap, clap,
> love, love, love, love,
> clap, clap, clap, clap,
> and a boom, boom, boom.

Charleyne sings these last four lines in a soft rhythmic voice, a cross
between a rap song and a spiritual. She seems to be making up the
song as she goes along. She continues to repeat this rhythm, "Clap,
clap, clap, clap, love, love, love, love, and a boom, boom, boom," for
perhaps two minutes. As she does this, several children stand close
around her, stopping what they are doing to listen.

This week, Charleyne has made a breakthrough, and I know the
story can be acted out. From the dark place where the father and
daughter kill each other comes the transformation of both characters into a prince and princess. This story holds out the promise of characters moving from anger, terror, and loss to the kind of
strength and dignity that fairy tales offer. What inner strength this
child has to manage such huge feelings and events, and to do so in a

narrative. Her song is the first of its kind in this classroom, much as her princess/Dora story was on day two of storytelling and story acting in this classroom.

As Charleyne goes off to her next activity, I see Lawrence and Demetrius sitting at a table across from each other in silent parallel play. I pull a chair up close to Lawrence. He is back at school now four days, having been absent for two months with chicken pox and subsequent complications. He is content and focused. He plays with stacking colored plastic rings that are about two inches around and a half inch high. I look at the skin on his arms and hands. There are still signs of the bumps and his scratching that beleaguered him during the winter months. At one point his ring tower topples over, and the plastic circles fall on the floor. He happily gets up and crawls under the table to get them.

Lawrence seeks close physical proximity to others, yet is quiet and shy, not venturing into the middle of activities in the block-building area or art area. He leans on me but keeps building for several minutes. After his tower topples over, he builds stacks of four and five rings, lines them up beside the container, and says, "They the mom, the boy." It seems that a stack of two and three rings are one person. I ask him if he wants me to write down his story. He nods eagerly. I write with my right hand as he leans on my left arm with the plastic circles moving in front of him.

> There's a mom and a boy and they go to a party. They push. [He is making pushing motions. I am not sure what they are pushing.] One goes to the back [of the container, hiding from the others; he is acting this out as he dictates]. "You ain't see me now. You ain't see me now!" [Meaning that the one character is hiding]. He comes back.

Lawrence is done and is smiling. It was as if his characters were playing hide-and-seek. He picks up the rings, puts them away, and goes on to play with little animal figures in a bucket on the table.

Demetrius is sitting by Lawrence, playing with magnetic tiles, using them to build a castle. He has built a structure with a base of tiles, then walls, and triangles on top of the walls to simulate the roof. He speaks in a quiet voice with a running narrative about characters. Sometimes the structure falls but he calmly rebuilds it. He says yes when I ask if he wants to tell a story.

Demetrius is continuously improving his English skills, but I still have a hard time understanding him at times. I know "Poppy" is what he and his siblings call their father. I also know that a dragon is Demetrius's favorite character to role-play in any story. He wants a dragon to be in every single child's story, and he wants to play it.

> Poppy build a house. The dragon come. The dragon flies. Poppy and *mi hijo* live in the house.

Demetrius's use of *mi hijo* (my son) in this story provides insight into his developing voice as narrator while also becoming the character Poppy as he dictates.

Mrs. Miller calls: "Two minutes till cleanup!" Suddenly there are several children who want to tell stories. I reply, "I will write them down at snack time." Chantell insists that I do it before snack so it can be acted out. I tell her, "OK, but very short. I know you are good at that." I write quickly as Chantell dictates:

> Princess watch TV. The dinosaur get mad and eat the princess.

Arianna is right on her heels, also insisting on a story. As I see a few seconds' opening, I scribble as fast as I can.

> Once there was a princess who lived in a castle. The dragon ate the princess. She was crying and had to go to the hospital. The prince buy her flowers.

Lawrence is listening to Arianna and says, "I want to do a cowboy and horse story." We are out of time, so I show him as I write his name and "cowboy story" in my notebook. I assure him that he will tell this story next week, and the group will act it out.

I often get the feeling that the children find their way into productive play activities each day and do not always feel inclined to turn it into a story until they are given the two-minute warning before cleanup. Then they crowd around whichever teacher is available for a turn to dictate as if they know this is a way to capture and extend their play.

Mrs. Miller starts singing "Miss Mary Mack." As the children move to the rug, Mrs. Miller points to open places in the circle for them to sit as she keeps the tune going. When she is done, we act out one nursery rhyme with our fingers: "Jack be nimble, Jack be quick, Jack jumps over the candlestick." Then Mrs. Miller says, "We are ready to act out stories. Mrs. McNamee will help us."

The children are squirmy and talkative. I come prepared to keep the pace moving with each dramatization succinct. We act out each story in the order that it was taken down. Sometimes this makes a difference—the group can see story ideas evolving as some storytellers listen to the narrative of the one before and fashion a narrative that responds to or expands on what they have just heard. For other children, their story concepts have been in mind for days and nothing can dislodge the idea they have to convey.

On some days, I tape-record the dramatization of the stories to note the timing and listen for the children's comments. Today's stories take exactly ten and a half minutes to act out. Timing helps me consider how manageable the dramatization activity is in terms of the other curricular activities being carried out. On this day, which has more dictated stories than any day so far, the timing was as follows.

Carlos: 3 minutes, 15 seconds
Miguel: 39 seconds
Charleyne: 3 minutes
Lawrence: 70 seconds
Demetrius: 30 seconds
Chantell: 40 seconds
Arianna: 40 seconds
Total: 9 minutes, 9 seconds
Final comments to the group before transition to washing hands: 40 seconds

I ask the authors when they dictate a story to pick which character they are going to play. This keeps the logistics during dramatization to a minimum. The teacher keeps track of where she left off in the circle of children in requesting actors for the next part to come along. Often a number of children long to play a favorite part: several boys will want to play dinosaurs or dragons, and all the girls inevitably want to play the princess. In such moments, I often invite children who want to play a part into the middle of the rug—the stage. The children in this class readily accept this accommodation. They cannot stand to be left out when I say, "No, so-and-so is the dragon," and they are equally appreciative if I allow anyone interested to come into the story. Most of the time, the stage is a bustling flurry of actors.

Due to time constraints, I do not read any of the children's stories all the way through at the group time before we enact the story. Every second counts in such a short school day (three hours door-to-door), and the children's attentiveness is at stake. I reread stories right after the child dictates one so that the author and those around us have heard it all the way through once, and can add or edit as needed. I also now have anyone standing nearby act it out right there in the moment. The children's stories grow in clarity and sureness from each moment spent focusing on enacting an idea.

The dramatization of each story brings new insights to the group's learning. Carlos's Batman story set a good pace for this group time. Carlos was Batman, Lawrence was Robin, and Demetrius was the Joker. I begin narrating, "Batman went in his car . . ."

"I'm making hats," Lawrence responds. "And a cowboy hat."

Lawrence loved the hat making at the art table earlier that day and insisted that I take one home when we finished cleanup time. I did not remember this comment until I replayed the recording later at home. This is the kind of detail a teacher will miss in responding to the rapid-fire needs of many children in the moment. Lawrence had dictated his story early in the day and then gone on to work at the art table making hats. The idea of a cowboy hat must have come up there. At cleanup time, he had asked if he could tell a cowboy story. I wrote in the story notebook that he would do this the following week, and he followed through. That narrative would wait a whole week before it came to full realization. But for the moment, I continue on without giving this comment any attention.

"... And Robin went in Batman's car. They went together."

I encourage the boys to pretend to drive in the car.

"They drove to the Joker," I continue. "And they fight with the Joker." When Mrs. Miller prompts Lawrence to pretend to fight with the Joker, he approaches Demetrius and punches him in the stomach. Demetrius is startled and starts to cry. Lawrence seems surprised.

Mrs. Miller immediately hugs and soothes Demetrius while I remind Lawrence about acting. "Lawrence, you just pretend, OK? Pretend like this. Watch Carlos. Carlos, show him how to pretend hit." Carlos does so. "Remember Carlos. Just pretend." I continue on. "They escape. Then what happened, an explosion happened in the car...."

Lawrence's long absence from school is evident in this scene; he is lacking the other children's deep familiarity with story staging and the safeguards of pretending. Lawrence shows us how far his classmates have come with these skills of thinking and mental discipline, and reminds us of the ground he is now regaining after his two-month absence. The group, with the teacher's directives, willingly reminds him and he quickly obliges. Lawrence would not hurt a flea; a story role called for an action, and he carried it out with one oversight: the need to pretend. This is just within his grasp, as is the idea of becoming a cowboy that he holds for another week.

In acting out the next story, Miguel's, Carlos—a role model for Miguel as he dictated a story in the hallway, his second for this year—has a flash of insight. He is now going to be the one to gain from the storytelling experience.

"I wanna be Robin! I wanna be Robin!" Carlos calls as I'm about to read Miguel's Batman story.

I point out that Batman's father appears in this story: "Batman flies with the guy who was his dad."

Carlos pauses before exclaiming, "Hey, I heard that one! I heard him!"

I stop, recognizing that he is figuring something out. No one says a word. He is realizing that he heard Miguel dictate this story about two hours earlier. I'm not sure whether he thought Miguel's story would be integrated into the one he had dictated, or just continue his line of imagery. But Batman flying with his dad was not something he had thought of; Miguel had brought that new detail to the narrative. Now it sunk in for Carlos what was happening.

"Yes, you did," I affirm, then, directing Miguel, I say, "Fly, Batman. Whoosh, there he goes!" As Batman flies around in a circle, I continue reading Miguel's story. "And then Batman fights with the king." José agrees to play the king, and the boys reinforce the idea of pretend fighting for Lawrence. I conclude, "Batman flies with all his friends," and the boys swoop around the carpet.

These thirty-nine seconds of acting are saturated with meaning for Carlos. I sense that Carlos had a new perspective and realization about what was written on the notebook page. He is realizing that there are a set of words that represent his thinking, and a set that are Miguel's. Miguel told a slightly different story. Carlos is also realizing that in his effort to help his friend tell a story, he acquired a new idea for his own future stories. He had not fully realized that Miguel had taken his Batman idea and extended it a bit further, with Batman flying with his dad. Carlos took a new story possibility away from the day's story acting. In his next story, which he tells when I visit two weeks later, there is a dad.

The lesson on pretend fighting for Lawrence fit well into the flow of events, and shows how much learning has taken place with the rest of the class. Lawrence's teachers and classmates make sure he gets back in stride with the community of actors who know how to visualize and enact ideas while listening and thinking, not hurting and distancing themselves from one another or school.

Charleyne's story follows. I introduce it by saying, "Now we have Charleyne's story. This one is amazing. It's like a fairy tale. Charleyne, are you the mom carrying her baby?" She comes to the middle of the circle with a big smile on her face. I continue, "We need a dad who is going to turn into a prince." Demetrius is sitting next to Charleyne and jumps up, saying, "I'll be the dad with a dog." I tell him there is no dog in the story. Charleyne says, "That's OK. The dad can have a dog." Her generosity to a classmate comes through once again.

We begin the dramatization. When we get to the numbers the dad likes, I say to the group, "Count with the dad: one, two, three, four, five..." I say each number slowly and clearly. The group counts with the dad and daughter as if the numbers have a magical meaning. When we get to fourteen, I put my hand up to signal: "Stop!" I show the children the piece of paper with the numbers written out that Charleyne had dictated. I want the children to see numbers in a story just like they usually see words. We continue on with the dramatization.

I then pause to warn the children, "The girl and her father are going to kill each other, but then they turn into a prince and princess. This is the part that is like a fairy tale. Watch how this happens. Charleyne and Demetrius, remember, we are just going to pretend to kill." They act this out. Next is the princess's song. I point to Charleyne. She breaks into her song and the group listens, silent and motionless. When she is done, I tell the group, "Charleyne wrote this story and a song, our first song. Great work! Now we have our last three stories..."

The children have no trouble staying glued to the action of this longer, more involved story. I was not worried about the tragic events because I knew, and explained to the children, that the characters transformed into prince and princess, and that the princess's song was coming. Charleyne had carried the audience through to a place of psychological safety.

Lawrence's story comes next. He moves into the middle of the circle with a shy grin. I call to Edythe sitting next to him to come be the mother. Edythe rarely speaks in class but is a willing actor in this story. I narrate, "There's a mom and a boy, and they go to a party." Both children take a few steps walking forward in the circle. "Now, Lawrence, remember how they push? Just *pretend* to push." I model what I saw him do at the table with the plastic pieces. He and Edythe mimic the action without saying a word. I tell Lawrence, "Now comes the part where you hide from your mother. 'One goes to the back.' Walk in back of me, Lawrence," I whisper, guiding him with this stage direction. "Now you say to your mother, 'You ain't see me now! You ain't see me now!'" Lawrence is smiling. He speaks up in a singsong voice, editing his own words, "You can't see

me! You can't see me!" I complete the narration, "He comes back."
Lawrence comes from behind me to stand next to Edythe. Both are
smiling, waiting for their next cue. I tell them, "Good story. Now it
is Demetrius's turn."

Lawrence and Edythe turn to sit down, but Carlos shouts out,
"Do it again! Do it again!" Something about this simple storyline
caught his interest. Before I can say anything, Lawrence crawls right
back into the circle and Edythe follows. This is not a problem, because the story takes fifteen seconds to act out. I reread the brief
narrative, and Lawrence and Edythe carry out their parts with sureness. In this encore, Lawrence says without prompting, "You can't
see me!" He shows that he is listening to the words, rhythms, and
grammar of classroom conversation. The daily practice of speaking
while enacting scenes from storybooks of all kinds is helping tune
his ear to the conventions of English as represented in the dialect
of the school.

The group time continues with performances of stories from
Demetrius, Chantell, and Arianna, all completed in less than two
minutes. Demetrius agrees to have two dragons, a character the
children love acting out, in his story. When it's time for Chantell's
story, she comes to the center of the rug. I narrate, "The princess
watch TV." She sits with grace and poise. She then says, "Did you
forget the dinosaurs?" I say, "No, that comes next." This tiny moment shows us the certainty of what children have in their minds
about the scene they want to portray in writing, and their uncertainty about what we teachers have committed to paper. It points
to the importance of the teacher listening carefully and loyally recording children's ideas. Their learning is rooted in trust. Pablo is
ready to eat the princess in disciplined pretend-gobbling actions.

Mrs. Miller and Mrs. Ortiz's community of three- and four-year-
old writers and readers are carrying out basic activities that have
meaning and purpose that these children understand. The activities
require the full use of the tools of the trade: ideas, the alphabet,
words, sentences, organization, and voice. With this community
of friends participating in basic literacy activities, we can see how
teachers create the context for their longer-term development as
readers and writers. The learning in storytelling and story acting is

the kind Vygotsky would herald—everyone grows and changes as a result of interaction with others who reflect a wide variety of skill levels, the most gifted as well as the beginner. When Carlos helped Miguel take the beginning steps of storytelling, he too made his own big steps forward. None of the steps would have happened without dramatization. In the enactment of stories, teaching and learning derive from the focus on each child inside of a tightly structured support that is responsive to and a springboard for the student's next step. The fact that everyone participates and watches allows all to benefit from each child's learning. In the next chapter, we examine how children progress from storytelling and story acting toward the more familiar image we seek in school: students reading books and writing in journals and notebooks independently.

Chapter 6

Looking Ahead to First Grade

Many of the public schools Mrs. Miller's children will attend use balanced literacy to guide instruction in learning to read and write. Based on the work of New Zealand educator Marie Clay, the balanced literacy curriculum framework was introduced to this country by the Ohio Literacy Collaborative in the late 1980s and furthered by the publication of *Guided Reading, Good First Teaching for All Children* by Irene Fountas and Gay Su Pinnell (1996). Balanced literacy provides an opportunity to illustrate how Vygotsky's and Mrs. Paley's ideas for preschool and kindergarten position children for learning to read and write independently during the primary years.

Fountas and Pinnell made an important contribution to the field of early childhood education when describing the threshold in development from being a nonreader to a fluent reader during the years from kindergarten through third grade. Guided reading, and the larger framework it is situated in, lets teachers envision how the many components of knowledge and skill with language and print begin to coalesce in kindergarten, before children grow articulate in speaking, listening, reading, and writing in the primary grades.

Balanced literacy is a curriculum with materials, methods, and assessments for teachers to use in coaching beginners as they take their first steps into the print world as independent readers and writers. An important premise in balanced literacy is that teachers

Reading Writing

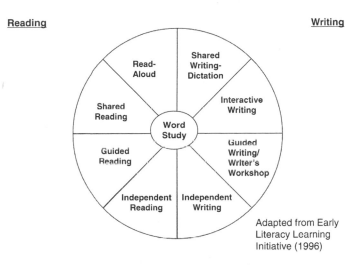

Adapted from Early
Literacy Learning
Initiative (1996)

Figure 3: Balanced literacy approach

are working with developmental tendencies that are unfolding over
a period of months and years in six- to eight-year-olds. Balanced
literacy includes eight components in the primary grades. Figure 3
presents these components as illustrated by the Ohio Literacy Collaborative, with a few modifications.

Of the eight balanced literary components, four address reading and four address writing. In the area of reading, teachers *read
books aloud* to children several times a day and also engage in *shared
reading*, where children recite together nursery rhymes and favorite
books, such as "Caps for Sale" or "The Three Billy Goats Gruff,"
that they have memorized after hearing them read so often. During
the school day, the teacher leads small-group *guided reading* sessions, coaching the children in practicing new reading skills from
carefully chosen texts at the appropriate level of challenge. Finally,
there is time for children to *independently read* library books as well
as books selected by the teacher.

In the area of writing, parallel activities complement the reading sequence. There are daily *shared-writing* routines where the
teacher writes messages and stories with children to demonstrate
the purposes and practices of writing. During the day, the teacher
creates opportunities for children to write in what is called "sharing

the pen," an *interactive* exercise in which children undertake writing tasks in concert with the teacher's support. During the day, as with reading, there are small-group *guided-writing* sessions to support children's developing skills in understanding and practice in being a writer—how writing works and how writers think and get help. Finally, the classroom offers opportunities for children to *write independently* for the full variety of purposes they invent and the teachers offer.

At the center of figure 3 is a circle I have added, "Word Study," as a reminder that the goal of these various activities is to increase the child's attention to words: building vocabulary, noticing how other authors pick and choose words, learning spelling patterns, and figuring out unknown words. Placing "words" at the center of the diagram reflects Vygotsky's belief that words are the mediator between us and the world we seek to reference. As six-, seven-, and eight-year-olds, children are at an age where they notice and use language in new ways. As Judith Lindfors (1987) discusses, this is the age when children are intrigued with jokes, secret codes, and inventing languages. As children come into the primary grades, they show us their fascination with language as a code, as a symbolic system that is invented and manipulated for conveying meanings. Instruction and guidance in learning to read and write capitalize on this fascination with words and how they work.

Balanced literacy offers several important sources of support to young children in the primary grades. First, it focuses on the oral-language foundations for literacy learning. It assumes that children are surrounded by and participate in daily conversations about experiences and ideas derived from books and personal experiences.

A second important feature of balanced literacy is the principle of "gradual release of responsibility." Jerome Bruner calls it "the hand-over" principle within a Vygotskian framework whereby adults gradually hand over to the child the skills and means for carrying out the activity more independently and, in this case, doing the actual reading and writing. As Bruner summarizes, adults contribute to "'setting up' the situation to make the child's entry easy and successful and then gradually pulling back and handing the role to the child as he becomes skillful enough to manage it" (1983, 60).

When reading aloud to children, the teacher is doing the reading. In shared reading, adult and child are reading together. When children read a book on their own, or pretend to read, they are moving toward more self-initiated skills and reading competence.

In setting out this array of activities, the balanced literacy framework acknowledges that there are multiple activity formats a child engages in daily over a period of years when becoming a reader and writer. In the process of guiding early readers, teachers take on different roles: modeling, supporting, coaching, and ensuring time for children's independent practice. From this framework educators have designed a comprehensive blueprint of classroom activities that support children's learning across the school day and week as children move toward proficiency as independent writers and readers with ever-increasing skill and sophistication.

Guided reading is designed for first- through third-grade instruction. However, as with other educational practices in the past decade, its activities and assessments have been extended downward to kindergarten and preschool. Thus we now hear about "guided reading groups" for kindergarten and even preschool. Herein lies the problem: preschool children are developmentally not ready for interacting with books and print in the same ways children ages six and seven are. What can and ought balanced literacy mean for young children aged three, four, and five?

Balanced literacy for preschool and kindergarten recognizes the oral-language underpinnings of development and the developmental transformations in the use of language for children between the ages of two and a half and six that learning to read and write derive from. Distinct and unique teaching practices are needed to guide literacy learning through the preschool and kindergarten years. Children have different developmental needs during these years as compared to primary-school-age children, and, as a result, literacy content and methods look different.

In many aspects of young children's development, early learning looks different from its more mature form. Story dictation and dramatization are good examples of literacy activities that illustrate this principle. Storytelling and story acting rely on reading and writing, but the child is not doing the actual reading and writing.

Figure 4: Balanced literacy approach for preschool and kindergarten

However, the processes of carrying out the activities expose the child to reading and writing in ways that require the full resources of oral-language interaction, the child's imagination and thinking, and the sound system of language and its translation into print conventions. Thus, participation in story dictation and story-acting activities—along with read-alouds, singing, nursery rhymes, and an introduction to the alphabet—prepare children for ownership and mastery of the symbolic resources of written language. Children are learning basic skills inside of basic activities.

Figure 4 provides a representation of balanced literacy for preschool and kindergarten that takes account of this developmental principle and prepares the children for full participation in the components as set out and implemented by Fountas and Pinnell by the time they are in first grade. As developmental theory and Vygotsky in particular will remind us, the pathway to first grade will not follow a neat linear progression of skill acquisition, but rather requires a reorganization and transformation of the child's approach to stories and what they are made up of—words—in arriving at the doorstep of independent decoding and writing.

Balanced Literacy for Preschool and Kindergarten

Balanced literacy for preschool and kindergarten children begins with the central organizer for language and eventually literacy development: stories. Stories for this discussion are a narrative account of events: they can be factual or fiction, but they are verbal. They are thinking that is expressed in words: recounting an event, telling a joke, making up a set of events with characters, or explaining a phenomenon.

Storytelling happens in conversation, while becoming a character in pretend play, when dictating a story to a teacher or older student, and when a child is an actor in a dramatization. Storytelling around the world follows different conventions and purposes in communities, but all people tell stories. All languages afford people the chance to talk about the past, present, and future and possible, hypothetical, and pretend worlds. As such, stories—narrative uses of language—are the starting point in schooling.

Reading and producing written accounts of all kinds are goals of schooling. Reading and writing help us capture every facet of human knowledge to represent it to ourselves in a way that helps us notice, think about, and change how we interact with the world around us. We write songs, equations, novels, diaries, blogs, and theories to capture how the world works. Using what others tell them in combination with what they imagine, children are creating narratives in their minds about who they are and what is happening in the world around them.

Vivian Paley recognized from her own listening and observing that children take their biggest steps forward in all areas of development when they are in play. When she moved from kindergarten to preschool to learn more about the development of play and storytelling that flourished in her kindergarten classrooms, she discovered:

> If, in the world of fantasy play, four- and five-year-olds may be called characters in search of a plot, then the three-year-old is surely a character in search of a character.

Place this three-year-old in a room with other threes, and sooner
or later they will become an acting company. Should there happen
to be a number of somewhat older peers about to offer stage direction and dialogue, the metamorphosis will come sooner than later.
The dramatic images that flutter through their minds, as so many
unbound stream-of-consciousness novels, begin to emerge as audible
scripts to be performed on demand.

The characters and plots are there, waiting, always in the process
of becoming. (1986, xiv)

The first responsibility of the early childhood curriculum is the
development of young children's oral-language skills. With stories
and oral-language development broadly writ as the centerpiece of
preschool and kindergarten, we can now touch base with each sec-
tion of the balanced literacy model to understand the pattern of
interactions that support children's entry into the varieties of storytelling we seek with them in reading, math, science, and the arts.

The activities of independent reading and writing set the stage
for children becoming the writers and readers that we aim for. Preschool and kindergarten classrooms now pay close attention to the
placement and arrangement of books, paper, and pencils in the
classroom, as well as the timing and patterns of children's comings
and goings from them. Children invent and discover life in school
with these materials when they are integrated with daily play as well
as in the foreground of daily classroom routines.

For the reading side of the activities, as with older children, read-
alouds stretch children beyond their current proficiency to think
about new ideas and experiences. Research has confirmed the place
and value of reading to children. Comprehension and vocabulary
grow exponentially when children are read to from a young age.
The parallel and complementary experience for writing with young
children is dictation. As it takes a reader to read aloud to the child,
likewise young children need someone who can do the writing to
record their ideas. Then the young child has the opportunity to
compose material and articulate ideas while someone else does the
transcription work. This is the hard work of being a writer, and
children can participate in it, just as they can comprehend when

listening to read-alouds. As we have seen in Mrs. Paley's and Mrs. Miller's classrooms, children as young as three are eager to begin representing their ideas in writing when there are willing scribes.

In shared reading, children along with their teacher are basking in the richness of written language together as they recite nursery rhymes and poems, sing songs, and read memorized editions of favorite books together. Through such daily experiences, children build a wide repertoire of cultural imagery, lyrics, tones, and beats to language and discern interesting word patterns. This repertoire of literary language committed to memory provides a deep well to draw from in reading experiences.

When children hear narratives such as *Goodnight Moon* by Margaret Wise Brown (1975), they can savor the references to two nursery rhymes:

> In the great green room, there was a telephone and a red balloon. And a picture of the cow jumping over the moon. And two little kittens and pairs of mittens . . .

The cow jumping over the moon references the nursery rhyme "Hey Diddle Diddle," and the kittens with pairs of mittens reminds us all of the return of order at the end of the day.

References to these nursery rhymes help young children connect with the bunny's preparation for bedtime. Brown provides an entrée for a new generation of readers into centuries of playful literary images that will continue to grow and expand. Like adult authors, children themselves are listening to, borrowing from, and trying out words and phrases as they invent their own stories in play and dictate them to their teachers.

In interactive writing, teachers make room for young children's wish to take up the pen and participate in the writing enterprise alongside more capable hands. When teachers have a flexible mindset about who holds the pen and is making the marks on paper, children readily experiment, practice, and pursue their own attempts at creating squiggles, drawings, and, in time, their own versions of writing.

As we examine further the continuum of story experiences that will benefit preschool and kindergarten children, we come to dialogic reading and additional dictation. These are the areas where, in the primary grades, teachers are offering what are called readers' and writers' workshops, guided reading groups where teachers provide coaching for novice readers and writers. It is these areas that educators stand to make the biggest error with preschool and kindergarten children. School administrators and teachers assume that these children can benefit from the kind of instructional goals, content, and formats that are appropriate for school-age children a year or two older. Instead, what preschool and kindergarten children need is someone more experienced reading to them in one-on-one or small group settings, and taking down their ideas in dictation.

Reading to young children and additional opportunities for dictation are areas of classroom activity that stand to benefit from parents, volunteers, and older children in elementary-school classrooms who can become partner or buddy readers and writers with preschool and kindergarten children. Half-day and even full-day programs are limited in how many reading and writing activities they can offer children in school. Resourceful teachers and school administrators will see a variety of ways to mobilize people of various ages and backgrounds to join the classroom to read to children and take down their dictations. Having middle school and high school students, grandparents, or volunteers from a community organization regularly visit Head Start classrooms can provide support, friendship, and help in bringing more competent others into the daily literary life of young children while they are in school.

Experiences in being read to provide children with one insight that cannot be acquired in any other way: what the rhythm and cadence of book language sounds like—its vocabulary and syntax. From daily read-alouds, they come to expect that the flow of words in books is very different than the flow of words in pretend play and everyday conversation at home or in school. They benefit from hearing the wide variety of ways that authors begin stories such as "Once upon a time" in order to know what to expect when they open a book. As Elizabeth Sulzby (1985) demonstrated, as well as the work of my colleague Joan McLane and myself (McLane and

McNamee 1990), this insight comes long before children learn to actually decode print; it develops as a function of being read to.

Dramatization is the all-encompassing activity in the balanced literacy model for preschool and kindergarten proposed here, encircling all of its eight components. Dramatization of stories in relation to all kinds of lessons is a necessary and essential part of learning in school for young children because it is synonymous with disciplined group behavior that relies solely on words and physical movement. Movement is the language of learning for children under the age of seven, and words are the symbolic medium school is foregrounding above all others.

Jerome Bruner reminds us that people have three ways of representing and communicating meaning:

1. Enactive modes of representation—physical resources including actions, gestures and movement
2. Iconic modes of representation utilizing visual images and resources
3. Symbolic modes of representation—words that are spoken, written, and signed in addition to mathematical and musical notation systems (1966, 1–29)

Schooling has its sights set on the third mode of representation; schooling seeks mastery of language and mathematical symbol systems. But current educational policy and practice are asking how soon we can get children to symbolic modes of mastery, and whether children need to play or dabble in any of the other modes of representation on their way to verbal and mathematical proficiency.

As theory and experience tells us, most children can learn to read and write, and they do have to pass through the stages and experiences associated with each mode of representation in order to arrive at creative proficiency in their use of each in representing ideas. Given the full breadth of representational resources needed for mathematics, the sciences, the visual and performing arts, as well as English language arts, educators cannot afford to privilege one mode of representation over another, nor should we want to.

In child development, infants and caregivers first communicate by reading each other's gestures and actions (enactive). Before an infant's first birthday, pointing is used to reference objects or pictures to enhance the gestures and sounds in communication (enactive and iconic). Toddlers enter the phase of burgeoning verbal development in many middle-class communities, and in later years in a variety of cultures around the world given differing cultural expectations. When children arrive in preschool at age three or four, their verbal skills are brand-new in their repertoire of communication tools. As educators, we are eager to seize hold of these emerging verbal skills to strengthen and expand them toward written language. And yet the urge to capitalize on them at the expense of the other two modes of representation that shore up their learning will shortchange children's development. As wisdom tells us, "the farmer who's so eager to help his crops grow that he slips out at night and tugs at the shoots inevitably ends up going hungry" (Jackson 1995, 194).

When children act out stories, they are participating in written language using all three modes of representation described by Bruner. Written language is re-created in spoken words and in visually enacted scenes where every word is brought to life with the help of others. Each character and each facet of an idea has a physical, visual, and verbal representation. Dramatization of ideas is an activity format that holds out our highest expectations for the use of language in children's futures. It utilizes written language's communicative resources in a way that children comprehend and gravitate toward.

Dramatization is a quintessential example of a starting point for learning to read and write that does not resemble actual reading and writing. Dramatization of stories is also an activity that embodies Vygotsky's ideas for mechanisms of development that are both evolutionary and revolutionary. The activity provides daily practice in taking an idea from the immediate stream of consciousness and remaking it in words, watching and listening to each word needed to re-create it. Each experience of dramatization gradually yet forcefully alters children's stance toward words as they recognize that their daily thoughts and experiences can be captured in written as well as spoken form.

For Vygotsky and Mrs. Paley, pretend play and self-initiated activity along with teacher-led dramatizations are central and unifying experiences in young children's school days. They call into action the basic skills we seek for children. Skills are practiced in a way that Judith Lindfors describes as best suited to literacy learning. She uses James Britton's concept of practice as rehearsal for a performance that contrasts with practice as used in referencing the work of a professional—such as an attorney practicing law, or a doctor engaging in medical practice. Instead of imagining children as practicing basic skills in order to prepare for a future performance of those skills, we can alter our stance to one of describing children as readers and writers from the beginning who are engaging in the practice of being writers and readers at successively more complex levels of skill and participation, but always as members of a classroom community (Lindfors 1987, 253).

This new perspective on the practice of young children's learning does not mean that educators do not draw attention to skills along the way. What is new is the context and assumption about young children's learning. Their learning is not an accumulation of skills that in a year or two or three are put to use in decoding simple texts. Whether they are from families of economic advantage and cultural resonance or from poorer communities or cultural backgrounds whose language practices do not align with school, young children learn to read and write by being immersed in the practices of reading and writing from the start. Children of all backgrounds learn to read and write by reading and writing with the help of others.

Drama is an art form ideally suited for fostering the goals of schooling for children in preschool, kindergarten, the primary grades, and beyond. It is physical, it creates a visual representation of a mental image, it is verbally expressive, and it can be adapted to enacting all types of ideas. It creates a representation of an idea that a class of very young children can experience, respond to, and reflect on as a group and individually. This is what makes it unique: the opportunity to experience ideas simultaneously as an individual and as a member of a group. The sequence of children's stories told in one day, and over time, documents the classroom community as it is growing every single day.

Several lines of published research and practice extend and implement Mrs. Paley's storytelling and story-acting practices within public schools in London (Cremin et al. 2013), Houston (Cooper

1993), New York City (Cooper 2009), the Appalachian Moun-
tains (Green 2009), and Massachusetts (Katch 2001, 2003), as
well as Chicago (McLane and McNamee 1990; Chen and Mc-
Namee, 2007). In fall 2012, the Boston Public Schools began the
"Boston Listens" project, in which Boston kindergarten teachers
were trained in storytelling and story-acting practices to be implemented with children across the city. What kind of learning do
these endeavors yield?

From Three to Seven: Becoming Writers and Readers

In an African American community several miles from Green
Park Elementary, I had the opportunity to observe children whose
teachers have worked to include storytelling and story-acting activities in their Head Start, kindergarten, and primary classrooms.
Visiting their classrooms gave me the chance to see storytelling and
story acting at work in another public-school setting, and to see
how these activities can provide an entrée to becoming a writer. The
voice and fluency of young authors from other communities illustrate the benefits of storytelling and story acting for children three
to seven years of age.

I visit Rose Jacobs and her first-graders in February, many of
whom I have known since they began school in the community
Head Start program four years earlier. One boy, Randall, is back in
school after being absent for five weeks with a bad case of scabies.
His arms, hands, and palms are covered in scaly, dry, and scabbed
sores. He pulls a crumpled envelope with "Miss Jill" written on it
from his backpack. Grinning quietly and without a word, he hands
it to me. I open it eagerly. In his own neat, careful printing, he has
written the following story. His layout, spelling, and punctuation
are included here.

> Once there was a little girl
> named Jill She wanted
> two go to the fair But
> Her parents?
> wouldnet let Her

She was a nice Little girl
She Had Listen
allway to Her Parentes
Then Her Mom and
Dad Had change
There mind
For a good little
girl was she
Then when Shu
grew up she
was still a nice oil Lady

Several weeks earlier, I had heard from Mrs. Jacobs that Randall would not be in school until a doctor certified that he was no longer contagious. We all wondered how he might be managing out of school for so long. After discussing the idea with his teacher, I filled a plastic bag with supplies that might remind him of the storytelling, drawing, and writing activities that we carried out in school. The bag included miniature copies of Eric Carle's *The Very Hungry Caterpillar* (1969) and "The Three Little Pigs. " I added pens, colored pencils, a box of crayons, a packet of markers, several pads of notepaper, a packet of envelopes, Scotch tape, a small pair of scissors, and a glue stick. These materials had been part of his daily school life since he entered Head Start at age three. What Randall handed me that day was his version of a thank-you note in the form of a story that he made up about me. And he had done so in storybook language.

In the course of our work, I never told Randall or any of the children stories about my childhood. I was the one who listened to their stories and read them books. Randall's story is his imagined biography of me. He told his story in the language he associates with the world of storytelling that I am synonymous with. As Lisa Delpit (1995) might describe, Randall showed exquisite skill in code switching.

Four months prior to this, he gave me a storybook he had written called "The Night of the Living Dead." He wrote and illustrated this book using a pen on lined paper that he tore out of a spiral notebook and then glued together.

Cover: The Night of the Living Dead
Page 1: The monster got the little girl
Page 2: The Lady monster got the boye
Page 3: The monster ate the fat Boy
Page 4: The monster ate the fat Girl
Page 5: The monster got the fat girl

Each page was illustrated with a tall, skinny monster figure, sometimes with four arms, all with teeth hanging out of its mouth, hair sticking out at all angles, and a sinister grin. The boy and girl were half the size, plump, and had sad faces. He drew big round circles for the eyes with a dot in the middle conveying their terror.

Randall is a quiet, good-natured child whose voice is seldom heard over the chatter of others. His stories reveal a lively, vibrant boy's imagination, and his classmates love to act them out. The key to the ease with which he expresses himself, in both his home dialect as well as the English spoken and written in school, is his literary experience in Head Start, kindergarten, and now first grade.

Randall attended a community-based Head Start program that put a premium on oral-language development. Children were invited into conversations with teachers, parent volunteers, program staff, as well as each other from the moment they walked through the door. Randall and his classmates were read to daily, storybooks were acted out, and his own dictated stories were written down and dramatized. He has grown up in school with the nuts and bolts of written language as part of his daily routines. He knows the forms and features of the written symbol system including the alphabet, layout of words and sentences with punctuation, and the process of transposing words to paper.

Through these experiences, Randall has developed code-switching skills. He recognizes that his home dialect, dialect spoken in school, and that of the books read to him provide him with a distinct identity that shifts in vocabulary, syntax, and pattern according to whom he is addressing, the setting, and the purpose. His first-grade teacher, Mrs. Jacobs, and his Head Start teacher, Tiffany Arnold, modeled and noted differences between home dialect and the dialect the children heard their teachers speak, as well as that of the authors and characters in the books we read to them. Books such as Mercer Mayer's *Liza Lou* helped them discern the contrast between story characters using their home dialect and the narrative's conventional English.

Randall learned to participate in the full range of school activities using his home dialect while being introduced to school discourse patterns of conversation and instruction. Randall and his peers became more proficient with formal English through acknowledgment of and respect for their home language, exposure to and participation in formal English, the focus in conversation and dictation on the communication of meaning, and the recognition that form follows function in language learning. Children attend to and refine forms and features of expression in English over a period of years when there is respect for and interest in the different ways of conveying meaning.

Randall's first dictated story as a three-year-old was a list of the people in his family; he has two sisters.

My mommy. My daddy. My sister. My sister. My cousin.

As a four-year-old, he told stories of monsters with great chase scenes. His stories were surprises, as one could never guess what was in his mind given his cheerful, quiet demeanor, never fussing at requests or expectations set for him or the group.

It was a little frog named Chuckie. He got a dog name Kermie. He goin' to school with the dog an' he saw a rainbow monster. An' then he saw a ghost. He didn't have no eyes. Then he was in the kitchen and the ghoulie be there. Then a big giant ghoulie be in the kitchen. The fat ghoulie, he be chasin' them. An' he be hidin' under the table. Then the ghoulie turned into a ghost. It was King Kong outside and the monster was in the house chain them.

Randall was a vital, active participant in the community of storytellers in his Head Start classroom. One afternoon when Randall was about to turn five, I observed his teacher, Mrs. Arnold, leading the storytelling and dramatization with the children. Five stories emerged that Mrs. Arnold discussed with me later that day. The story sequence began with two children telling stories referencing characters from "Goldilocks and the Three Bears" that the children had been asking Mrs. Arnold to read over and over again. The more they heard the story together, and had time to play out its themes and their own variations, the more ideas they had about every detail referenced.

Shanica began that afternoon Head Start session with this story:

> The Papa Bear and the uncle sat down and looked at wrestling. And the baby bear have to go to school. The Baby Bear made him some friends. And the teacher whopped the baby Bear 'cause he was actin' bad and his mother came up to school. And he had come over to the auntie's house and stay all day. And he was getting tired from coming home. The mother was asking the uncle to come to her house tomorrow. The end.

Arianna told the next story, offering a version of the three bears that reflected events as they might take place in her doll corner version of the story, mixing pretend family life with the fairy tale.

> Mama Bear went to the store. Daddy Bear went to the store. The Baby Bear stayed home. Baby Bear went to the store on his own and he saw Mommy and Daddy Bear. So they both got into the car together. And the little girl went in the house. Baby Bear left the door open. She thoughted and thoughted. She wasn't hungry. She sat on Daddy's hard chair and she sat in Mama's hard chair and she sat on Baby's soft chair and she broke it. And the little girl was really upset. She slept in Daddy's bed, and Mama's bed. They all came upstairs and they all saw the little girl in Baby Bear's bed and they saw the chair was broke and she ran home. The end.

Arianna came to school that day in a bad mood. She said her mother had given her money to buy a candy bar on the way to school, but that her cousin took the money and she got nothing. When the children came to the rug for the initial large group meeting of the afternoon, Arianna was restless and fidgety. She kept taking her shoes off and on, nudging the child next to her to tie them, and then pulling away to loop the laces around into a bigger and bigger knot before taking her shoe off again. The teacher told Arianna to leave the group to sit on a chair so she could listen and stop interrupting the others. Arianna went to the time-out chair and sat, gazing out the window with a distant look in her eyes.

After the reading of "Goldilocks and the Three Bears," Arianna, along with the other children, went to pick an activity. Before she did, she told Mrs. Arnold, "Sometimes when you're mad and can't get what you want, you get mad. But then you get over it. That's what my grandpa say." She went on to play in the house area and then, twenty minutes later, came running to her teacher with a story she wanted to be written down. Mrs. Arnold later discussed the remarkable thoughtfulness of this child, her ability to collect herself and make good use of both the story she heard and the dictation that would be acted out with classmates to bring cohesion and meaning to her experiences that day.

Randall came to his teacher with a story that surprised everyone. It referenced an event that happened right outside the classroom door as he came to school that day and included a bear. Such a detail might be accidental, but it is also a thread of continuity as the children pick up the narrative line when it is their turn to tell a story.

When she came to Randall's story during the group time on the rug, Mrs. Arnold said to the class, "See if you can figure out what happened to Randall when he was walking across the schoolyard to our classroom today. Watch as he acts this out."

Once upon a time I saw a bird. He was running up in the air, and the bird came down. When he came down, he was dead. He was dead because he had fell. He had fell on the concrete. Then the bear came and he ate the bird up too. The end.

Randall acted out the bird's motions, and Tony took the part of the bear. Mrs. Arnold then said, "Randall, tell the children what happened to the bird." Randall replied, "He flew into the window." Mrs. Arnold said, "Yes, that happens. When we go outside today, we're going to look at the windows. Let's see if we can figure out why the bird flew into the window." Later, when they were outside, Mrs. Arnold instructed the children to look up at the school building windows, which reflected the clouds. Mrs. Arnold asked them what they could see, and why they could see clouds reflected in the glass. She asked them what the birds might be thinking. Everything that Mrs. Arnold notices in stories she brings back to group discussion.

The fourth story was Hugo's and seemed to be written by a wise, cultural elder authoring a book of fables. It reflects a child's imagination at its best, sensitive to life's vagaries even at this young age of four.

> The sun came out and it talked to the boy. It says, "Hi, little boy." The sun said, "I'll come out every day." The sun said, "The grass come out with the flowers. All different flowers." And then the father came and said to the boy, "Could you go to the store with me?" And the man said, "You might as well cook food because here comes the wolf."

As the children acted this out, they could all see the tranquility and order of a beautiful sunny day when everything is going well, and the sun is happily watching over all. But then there is a warning, someone reminds you to be prepared, as danger will surely come. Danger for young children often takes the form of a wild animal. In acting out these stories, they see that they can be the wolf or bear, or the one who is scared. Story dramatization on a daily basis gives young children plenty of opportunities to experience all sides of fear and every other emotion.

Evan's was the last story for that day.

> Mickey Mouse go with his girlfriend. Goofy came. He walkin' with Donald Duck. Then Mickey Mouse, his birthday was today. Then Donald Duck had an Easter egg. Then Goofy drivin' his car. A bird came. The bird made a house. And then he fly away. Mickey Mouse, he go for a walk. Donald Duck, he go with Big Bird. Then a red heart came. That's the end.

The children in this classroom love to act out stories, but this final one seemed to hold special meaning for them. At first glance, the story might seem like a listing of television characters coming and going without purpose, but as with all literary communities, the power of the narrative lies in the connections it makes for its listeners. These Head Start children, like all children, experience fear, uncertainty, and anger, as well as moments of happiness and contentment. The Disney characters embody certainty, happiness, and safety. Evan had been sitting at the story table playing with miniature plastic zoo animals as the other children told stories to the teacher. He had heard every story and references each of the authors. By depicting the activities of the Disney friends, he is filling the stage with school friends enjoying a good day.

Evan goes further; the gathering of friends who spend the day together is reinforced with reasons to celebrate. There is a birthday, and a reminder of Easter, and the holiday to celebrate friendship: Valentine's Day ("Then a red heart came"). Mrs. Arnold mentions these details as she guides them in acting out this story that brings such great pleasure to the group.

In Mrs. Miller's and Mrs. Arnold's classrooms, storytelling and story-acting activities give voice to the poets and writers in the children. The activities have an uncanny way of drawing out their collective expressions of friendship, comfort, humor, and wisdom that advance their growth toward literacy as a group of friends, not just as individuals. The children are finding their own voice as storytellers with one another, and as they listen to the stories the teacher reads and tells each day.

Another part of the achievement is that when the children are given time to play out the stories they bring with them to school, they willingly use part of this time to work in focused, sustained ways when the teacher is invested in listening to and writing down their stories. They freely engage in disciplined verbal and logical thinking.

The stories of Randall and his classmates from ages three to seven provide evidence of their interest and initiative in seeking out the written word to glean new insights and perspectives. We see this in the children's revisiting "Goldilocks and the Three Bears" as well as experiences they have had inside and outside the classroom. They demonstrate their command of different ways of using language in

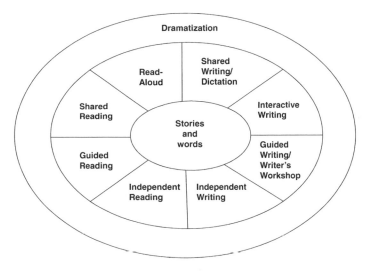

Figure 5: Revised balanced literacy model for primary grades

print, their different voices as writers, and their willingness to experiment with different literary genres long before they read and write independently.

Written language development hinges on our listening first to the stories and messages that children want to communicate. As we listen, children work hard to become clearer in their expressions, more resourceful and effective in articulating their thoughts. The desire to communicate is followed by their interest in mastering forms and features of the code that make such communication possible. Randall's ability to create a story using the literary language of the culture he knows his teacher and I come from is a testament to the listening he has been doing, and the sensitivity he brings to future learning.

Most teachers and curricula for kindergarten and the primary grades would be itching to get at Randall's grammar, spelling, and punctuation. The urge to clean up forms and ensure that spelling and punctuation are correct is a preoccupation in most classrooms because it focuses on the observable product. As with the development of oral language, effective educational practice needs to revise the focus of concern from form to content. Children care about forms and features of the written code as much as we hope they will, and they attend to them as they gain skills and mental focus to juggle these details alongside their motivation to write. In the meantime, stories that Randall and his classmates have been telling and acting out attest to the long-term commitment these children have to learning how to use print to read and write.

From preschool through first grade, Randall and his classmates navigate the transformation from speakers to writers within the balanced literacy framework, starting with stories and their dramatization in preschool, to reading and writing more independently in first and second grade. There is one modification that I would make to the original balanced literacy model offered by Fountas and Pinnell: maintain the place of story dramatization in daily reading and writing activities in the primary grades. This is depicted in figure 5.

The benefits of dramatization do not stop as children transition to more independent reading and writing. Just as children benefit from being read to through elementary school, they continue to benefit from someone else taking dictation as they work out new and more complex ideas they want to put on paper. The content they conceive as writers continues to grow more complex in advance of their physical skills in handwriting or typing. The need for and opportunity to examine their own ideas in print continues.

The opportunities for children's learning depend on the teacher's mastery in leading this basic activity. What teaching skills are involved when orchestrating learning through dramatization in classrooms with young children?

Chapter 7

Staging Stories

Some of the best days of school can also reveal vulnerabilities in a teacher's skill set. My time in classrooms alongside both experienced teachers and novices are not all shining examples of expertise. I continue to learn from my mentors: Mrs. Paley, Vygotsky, young children, their teachers, and my student teachers. All of them were with me in Mrs. Miller's and Mrs. Arnold's classrooms.

Many of my teaching skills are well developed, but those involved in leading dramatization of stories, the heart of the thesis regarding children's learning being put forward here, are still emerging. This is the teaching activity that has excited and challenged me the most, ever since I first observed Vivian Paley in her classroom. It is a prime example of a teaching-learning opportunity that is negotiated in the moment, in the active give-and-take of relationships among children and their teachers. Story-acting experiences reflect the rapport between teacher and children, and the balance of control teachers seek when they invite children's imagination, focus, and interest around the edge of a rug. It can be a precarious moment, and one where teachers often say, "Can't we skip this part?" Too much can happen that makes it seem like things are getting off track or out of control.

Consider the events from Mrs. Miller's classroom in late March, one week after Carlos and Miguel told their Batman stories that shaped other stories told that morning. The children resist wearing jackets; it is 45 degrees outside but feels like 70 under the blue sky and with the warm sun melting off the last bits of snow. The read-aloud for the day is Dr. Seuss's *Hop on Pop* (1963). The children are giddy with the rhymes and animated pictures emphasizing the meaning of the words, but they also show anxieties lurking under the surface.

> "UP PUP Pup is up.
> CUP PUP Pup in cup.
> PUP CUP Cup on Pup
> . . .
> PAT CAT Pat sat on cat.
> PAT BAT Pat sat on bat.
> NO PAT NO Don't sit on that.
> SAD DAD BAD HAD Dad is sad.
> Very, very sad.
> He had a bad day. What a day Dad had!"

Mrs. Miller stops and asks, "I wonder why Dad had a bad day?" Three children shout out responses. "I know, he shoot guns!" the first says. Another says, "He got fired." And a third says, "His house burned down." She comments, "Wow, yes, that's a bad day," and continues on.

At activity time, the sand table becomes the center of intense focus and arguments, perhaps because children seek out its soothing quality. Mrs. Miller spends considerable time monitoring the rotation of children there, helping them move on to other play areas as needed. Chantell wants a turn at a moment when the table is particularly crowded. She lingers, pouting and silent. When I pass by, she says excitedly, "Mrs. McNamee, let's go to the doll corner and you make a big mess and I'll yell at you!"

Chantell dashes into the doll corner and begins dumping clothes on the floor. I stop her as a few things go flying. "Chantell, tell the story. I'll write it down and we can act it out." I am rushing her into dictation to stave off the moment of chaos. She dictates.

> Dinosaurs like to eat all the dinosaurs. The princess come, two princesses. Thing 1 and Thing 2 mess up and destroy my house. The prin-

cesses let them destroy the house. Then the princesses open the door and say, "Get out of my house!" The Things do nothing else. The end.

I write slowly and deliberately to calm Chantell, my own racing heartbeat, and the frenzy of worry Dr. Seuss's characters from *The Cat in the Hat* can stir up. It works for a few minutes.

Soon Daniella, Maria, and Charleyne join Chantell, wanting to make pizza. They slap dishes onto the table, rattle off ingredients they need, and shout orders to one another: "Go to the store and get some sausage and cheese and pizza." "You get the babies, I'm going." "Get her a clean diaper, girl!" "Get some bologna and pepperoni!" "I gotta get the money. Give me all the cash." Chantell is enveloped in the baking drama, and things are no longer flying.

At a table a few feet away, Lawrence is trying to get small pattern blocks to stand up on the table to build the walls of an enclosed space. They keep toppling over. I remember that last week he had mentioned a cowboy during dramatization and wanted to write a cowboy story. I seize this moment to connect with that story idea and say, "Lawrence, remember last week you were thinking about a cowboy and wanted to tell a story about one for us to act out?" "Yeah," he says, and dictates the following narrative without missing a beat:

Cowboy. He can hop on the horse. He catched the monster. He don't touch the monster. The cowboy go back to his house. The horse can sleep in his room.

I do not know where he got the idea or the wish to tell this story, but it is his own narrative and waited a whole week to be told. It would not be his last cowboy story. It became one of his signature characters in dictated stories, and the group began to recognize how special it was when the horse got to sleep in the same room as the cowboy.

Daniella arranges several chairs in front of a magnetic easel and says she is playing school. She tells Maria, José, and Edythe to sit down in the chairs and pay attention, that she will teach them their lessons. She says, "Spell 'Sam I am'!" She then looks down at the tub of magnetic letters in front of her and studies them. She becomes absorbed in arranging letters in rows on the easel.

Maria, José, and Edythe sit staring at Daniella. After about two minutes, I ask Maria and José if they would like to tell a story. José does not say a word. Maria, who works hard at expressing herself in English, waves both of her hands in front of her and says, "Yes!" She says, pointing to José, "He speak no English." I tell her, "He can tell you the words and I will write them down." I notice that Carlos and Juan are arguing over who had the computer first and whose turn it is. Mrs. Ortiz is intervening to help the boys, so I know I have to handle translation issues with Maria. She is more than up to the task.

Maria and José start up a lively conversation, chattering back and forth excitedly. I sit next to them with pencil poised on the page. Maria turns and looks at the page and dictates line by line, translating for José. It is José's first story.

The prince trapped the dragons. The dragons eat the prince. The prince is in the mouth of the dragon and is trapped. The prince fights. The prince has four dogs.

Both children gesture and dramatize each phrase with their hands. I use present tense to keep things clear. We sit in this close and focused animated conversation for several minutes, savoring the images.

Maria then says, "He has more story." I glance around; no one is waiting to dictate so I gesture to them both, saying, "Go ahead." Maria continues to translate.

One horse. The horse jump. The bad boys bang with their guns. The horse jump with the prince. The prince is dead.

I am continually struck by the fact that so many of the children's stories have princes and princesses, castles, battles, and fighting for justice. There is a nobility to their narratives.

I then ask Maria if she has a story. She dictates.

There is a horse and two dragons. The dragons eat the horse. The bear is sleeping. The dad eat the bear. The mom goes to rescue the baby prince. There is a big explosion. The dragon and the bear is sleeping.

She captures themes in José's story, and ones from last week: the explosion from Carlos, and the horse from Lawrence. These are the signs of cross-fertilization of ideas in a literary community: taking up a character or theme and trying it out in one's own narrative train of thought.

Pablo listens to Maria and José. He tells Maria in Spanish that he wants to tell a story, and she agrees to translate again.

A car. Two cars. Fell at dark. The car crash. The pig fell on the car.

I repeat every word, Maria confirms, and Pablo, José, and Maria act it out as we go. "This sounds like a Dr. Seuss story," I say, just before the five-minute call for cleanup, and everyone hurries to the activity they want to squeeze into the final minutes of playtime.

After enough has been done to clear the rug area, Mrs. Miller calls for Jack: "Thumbs up! 'Jack be nimble, Jack be quick,'" she says, as the children squirm and fall over one another. One calls out, "My story, my story!" Charleyne insists, "No, my story first!" And Demetrius says, "I want to be the dragon!" Carlos does not want to leave the computer. Mrs. Miller gets a signal from Mrs. Ortiz that she is needed to speak with the school social worker. I take her place on the rug while Mrs. Ortiz rounds up the stragglers and prepares for snack.

I began to sing a new song with gestures: "My hat, it has three corners, three corners has my hat . . ." The children stare at me. They point around their heads as I demonstrate gestures that go with the song. I use the few seconds of focus to move right into the stories. "First story: Charleyne's."

Charleyne scrambles into the circle and starts to pick girls to be the two princesses. I put a halt to this. "Charleyne, no. That's the teacher's job. Come stand in the middle of the circle, and I will pick the actors." The children are leaning into the circle, many starting to play a character they want to be—a dog, a dragon, a princess—before even hearing the story. The story dramatization is blurring into a sort of puddle of their own imagery. The protocol we usually follow is not holding.

Within two seconds, I realize I can get angry and put a stop to everything, or I can work this through with the children. I know there had been a number of upsets during the afternoon and do not want to end the day with more. I decide to go with the semi-chaos of it all and bring goodwill to the setting. If this is the activity that demands my best skill, becoming angry is not going to mark an achievement. So I plunge in, and for each story, I allow the children to come onto the stage and play a character as they choose. I narrate in a clear director's voice to keep things moving.

When I get to Daniella's story, the last one with a prince and princess, no one will play the prince. The eight girls present that day are all on the stage becoming princesses in their minds. Daniella insists that a boy has to play the part and won't back down. I look around. None of the boys move. I ask Lawrence, who is next in line for a part; he says, "No." I sense the whole group is just done. On any other day, I would have had a discussion: "What can we do here? How can we act out the prince?" Today, the group has no reserves for discussion and problem solving. Instead, I say, "We will pretend there is a prince." I push ahead, narrating the final story of the day.

> One day there was a princess who had a beautiful prince and the princess was cheating at Angry Birds. There was a daddy and he loved to count numbers and do ABCs.

It is a good story to end on. The children love it. Why? The threads of other children's stories are in Daniella's: The prince and princess are Maria's favorite characters. There is the reference to a digital game, which has appeared in Charleyne's stories of late. The dad counting numbers in the last sentence references Charleyne's story of a week ago.

Daniella's story captures the rhythm of other children's imaginations alongside her own. This is what good play cultivates, as do the listening to and acting out of one another's stories. Daniella brings the stabilizing image needed to guide the group to the school day's "happy ending." In truth, it was difficult, but we were all smiling in the end. The decision to forge ahead with goodwill bore fruit from the activity itself and the children. Daniella saved the day, and I did not see it coming.

Becoming More Skilled

Why, we might ask, might a teacher push ahead with story dramatization if the children demand attention, with a need for their wishes to be heard during the enactment of scenes, forgetting the basic classroom routines and rules for group time on the rug? Why would any classroom teacher eagerly look forward to this time of day? The answer is because the children want it so intensely and the children benefit from it so much. Dramatization of dinosaur battles and crying babies are the heartbeat of the teaching-learning relationship in preschool and kindergarten classrooms.

If I had not read Vygotsky and only knew Vivian Paley, I would have said, "Mrs. Paley is an extraordinarily gifted teacher and 'this is her thing.' Theater is her particular form of teaching expertise. I can appreciate what she is doing, but I am going to leave that part to her, and just do what is comfortable for me." Mrs. Paley, however, reminds us in *Wally's Stories* that when dictation alone is offered in preschool and kindergarten, a few children, mostly girls, take up the invitation to participate. The rest of the children will comply when dictation of words to accompany a picture are required in a teacher-directed activity. Why does story dictation draw all children, and particularly boys, if dramatization was included?

This is where Vygotsky can help clarify the work of teaching and learning. Jim Wertsch (1981) points out that in Russian, a single word signifies both teaching and learning. As an English speaker, it is hard to imagine what it might mean to have such reciprocity described by one verb, but dramatization of stories is an activity that does just that in teacher-student relationships. It is an activity that exemplifies the give-and-take among friends in a zone of proximal development—*their* zone. As we see in Mrs. Miller's classroom, dramatization enables children to use storytelling in pioneering and transformative ways. It offers children the incentive to listen to one another, to what the teacher is presenting, and to their own streams of thought.

We are left with confronting the challenges that the activity poses for teachers and learning about the teaching skills involved. Without Vygotsky, it would never have occurred to me that teacher educators needed to uncover what's going on in dramatization and learn the skills to carry it out. As in all areas of teaching, effective skills need modeling and then practice. Teachers can become more effective over months and even years with modeling, coaching, and conversation about what is taking place.

I wrote to Mrs. Paley to describe challenges with dramatization of children's stories. She is an avid letter writer and responded, in a letter dated October 13, 2012, with detailed notes that speak to exactly who is learning what, both teacher and children.

> I am happy to discuss the important issue you bring up: the difficulty some teachers have in dramatizing the children's stories. As with any activity, if it does not seem to yield easily to the children's management, go back and start with the earlier, logically easier format.
>
> What, in fact, is this more simple format of which I write? It is the acting out of very easy books and scenes. My own kindergarteners, after all, were quite used to dramatizing books like "The Carrot Seed," "The Three Billy Goats Gruff," and much easier books, in choral style. (The only place, I think, where I refer to this is in *The Girl with the Brown Crayon*, 55.) In a preschool classroom, we practiced the acting out of scenes from books, going around the rug and giving pairs of children small scenes to act out, with specific directions from me or from the storyteller. Given a certain kind of restless kindergarten, this worked. I would do the same with older children.
>
> In other words, it is well to copy what theater people do: create exercises out of scenes, including scenes the teacher makes up. There is no reason for a teacher to allow story acting to get out of hand—or block play or doll corner play to fall apart. If a group seems to appear overly excited when acting out a story, then the activity must be reduced to some basic skills required by specific groups of children.

Sample directions:

Teacher: "I have noticed that our story acting goes best when there are three actors on the stage. Today we are going to act out a story from last year's kindergarten with three actors, and we'll go around the rug giving every group of three a chance to act out the story." (It is one easy concept.)

"The bunny walked slowly in the woods, looking all around for an adventure. It saw a little bear who was lost. 'I'll help you find your cave.' They walked and walked until they found Big Bear eating blueberries. 'Oh good, here is your lost bear cub.' 'Thank you,' says the mother."

If necessary, or if a teacher feels it is a good idea, every day, before story telling and story acting begin, the teacher can create a little story for three children at a time to act out, creating along the way very specific acting rules.

Actors need rules by which to act stories properly. (After a while, when children are allowed to act out their own stories, the group can keep up daily exercises in whatever format is deemed useful.) "Here's a good sentence for acting out in Peter's story. Let's practice it two by two, and then we'll do the whole story."

What I am suggesting here, of course, is nothing less than taking story telling and story acting seriously as theater. It gives us a logical reason to practice behaviors.

Another thought, when a story is being dictated, the teacher must feel free to say, "We'll stop here. This is just right for acting out." Remember, the teacher is in charge. These are acting exercises.

If in the doll corner, a doll is being tossed around, we do not need to yell at the "naughty" child. We do need to practice "putting the baby to sleep," "playing with the baby," "seeing if baby is hungry" etc. The teachers must break down good play and good story telling and story acting into scenes to be practiced. It goes without saying that there are dozens of scenes to be used for practice in almost any of Margaret Wise Brown's books, including even *Goodnight Moon*.

Mrs. Paley opens the way for both novices and those with more experience to see where skilled practice comes from, not only in dramatization but also in the monitoring of children's activity in all areas of the classroom throughout the school day. She helps us see how teachers can meet the imagination of children in play, storytelling, and story acting with a vision of her teaching goal: well-acted scenes of all kinds, but not ones where children hurt one another, themselves, or their families. She sets out a curricular path for teachers and student teachers to copy and practice.

Understanding Teaching

Vygotsky must have had some inclination of the teaching possibilities Mrs. Paley describes to come up with such a remarkable theory, but this was not his professional focus. His work was describing the blueprint for a new way of understanding young children's learning and subsequent development. Learning unfolds in interactions with adults and/or peers. From their experiences, children gradually come to recognize, control, and manage their actions in proactive ways. The child is the last to realize what he or she has been in fact learning, what message about expectations is to be derived from patterns of experience (Vygotsky 1981, 162).

Vygotsky offers several ideas about learning in zones of proximal development that can help us understand what is important for teachers in Mrs. Paley's lesson plan on dramatization of stories.

Imagination. Along with other psychologists studying human development, Vygotsky realized that at roughly age two and a half, a profound new mental activity becomes possible: pretend play. It is a breakthrough to a new form of thinking: considering the possibility of a situation, a person, or set of actions that do not exist in the immediate present. Vygotsky notes,

> Imagination is a new psychological process for the child; it is not present in the consciousness of the very young child [infants and toddlers], it is totally absent in animals, and represents a specifically human form of conscious activity. (1978, 93)

The imagination heralds a new era in development, separating infants and toddlers from preschoolers and all who follow. This is what educators value—for example, in the Common Core State

Standards—but are unsure how to capture and capitalize on. Too quickly, educators are drawn to facts and skills before turning to thinking, which sometimes we delay addressing for years until reading and writing skills are fully developed—to the detriment of their thinking and verbal skills.

Vygotsky cautions that not every ungratified wish in a child's life can result in play. However, when there is time and room for play, children stretch themselves to transform a wish into a possibility, a rough draft of what the scene might look like if it were to happen. Mrs. Paley shows us how teachers can guide children's inclinations to play toward more full-scale lines of thinking and reasoning with others in words. As Vygotsky emphasizes, "In play a child creates an imaginary situation" (1978, 93). Creating requires conscious, active construction work.

Rules. Vygotsky spent considerable time in detailing a central attribute of play: that it has rules.

> One could go further and propose that there is no such thing as play without rules. The imaginary situation of any form of play already contains rules of behavior, although it may not be a game with formulated rules laid down in advance. The child imagines himself to be the mother and the doll to be the child, so he must obey the rules of maternal behavior....
>
> Sully early noted that, remarkably, young children could make the play situation and reality coincide. He described a case where two sisters, aged five and seven, said to each together, "Let's play sisters." They were playing reality.... The vital difference, as Sully describes it, is that the child in playing tries to be what she thinks a sister should be. In life the child behaves without thinking that she is her sister's sister. In the game of sisters playing at "sisters," however, they are both concerned with portraying their sisterhood; the fact that two sisters decided to play sisters induces them both to acquire rules of behavior. Only actions that fit these rules are acceptable to the play situation: they dress alike, they talk alike, in short, they enact whatever emphasizes their relationship as sisters vis-à-vis adults and strangers.... What passes unnoticed by the child in real life becomes a rule of behavior in play. (1978, 94–95)

Vygotsky helps teachers notice what is important about the forward-moving thinking that children are engaged in as they negotiate roles and actions in their play scenarios together. The unfolding of play into a satisfying scene is not a given; on the contrary, it has to be achieved. Vivian Paley's work has been widely acclaimed because she portrays how the youngest children in school take each idea that comes to them and put it into an invitation to others to think along with them. She shows us the gradual daily work of children developing their imaginations with one another, in a reciprocal negotiation of the premises of a pretend world, a hypothetical possibility. They have to accept the premises of one another's proposals to take the scene forward together, using words, actions, and imagination.

Practice with others. Vygotsky, like all other scholars studying human learning and development, recognized that learning and development do not happen in one experience or one well-formulated lesson. Time for practice means lots of trial and error over the contours of days and weeks amid other life circumstances and routines. Vygotsky's rationale is helpful because in describing children's learning within activities, not separate from them, he provides us with a lens for seeing each day as a new draft, a new approximation of the thinking, speaking, and acting children can achieve. He reminds us that adults and peers participate in each child's learning.

Tomorrow's Teaching

If Vygotsky had seen Mrs. Paley at work, he would have singled out dramatization of stories as an instantiation of what he had in mind for learning in a zone of proximal development. This classroom activity would have become a favorite, because it epitomizes learning in the nebulous yet certain and necessary interactions among friends as they draw one another into the activity. The work of playwrights, creating stories to be acted out, is a disciplined, rule-bound crafting of the imagination in words that benefits others as well as oneself.

The teaching skills involved in working in an individual's as well as a group's zone of proximal development can be learned—

and taught. Dramatization of stories is one of the best examples we have of zones of proximal development in action, which is why it is worth studying. Teachers know they cannot simply let a group of children interact in open-ended ways. They build a group structure, a community ethic, and set of practices that are managed in a way that illuminate the children's opportunity to offer ideas to the group—and the group's responsibility to and encouragement of each individual child. Story dramatization provides a curriculum for teachers to work on these professional skills.

Vygotsky's view of storytelling and story acting point to the unique and important contribution that teacher and children bring to this balance of the individual and group in learning. As Vivian Paley came to recognize, storytelling and story acting enable teachers to come as close as they can to listening to a child's imagination translated from play into a story. Within a few minutes, the teacher can unlock an individual child's imagination and build a two-way bridge between the mental life of each individual child with that of the group as his or her story is acted out. As we have seen in children such as Lawrence with his cowboy stories, Mrs. Miller's students are sure of their trains of thought. They develop ideas over time that are revealed in their stories, ideas that would otherwise have no expression in school, or perhaps anywhere, if it were not for the interest and expectation of the teacher. With storytelling and story acting, children learn that school is a place for ideas, a place to articulate and record them so that others can learn about them, add to them, and connect to the full array of ideas that school can open up to authors.

Dramatization is difficult to carry out; it is the part of Vivian Paley's work that teachers would rather leave out because children can seemingly get out of control. The activity looks simple and straightforward, but it gets messy very quickly. Most teachers readily agree that the stories children dictate are interesting and even remarkable. What can be frustrating is the fact that the best way to tap into the children's inventiveness and harness it for school learning is to act out their stories. The challenges in leading dramatization serve to remind me of those areas in my teaching where I need to observe myself and the children more closely and practice. Viewing story acting as a core teaching activity in preschool, kindergarten, and the primary grades draws attention to fundamental professional teaching skills: opening up children's lives to content in all curricular areas, assessing and accounting for learning, building a community that honors the children and their families, and providing guidelines for conflict resolution. What do storytelling and story acting have to do with these elements of professional teaching?

Chapter 8

Starting Points for Teachers

It is a warm day in late April. The Head Start children in Mrs. Miller's classroom are on their way out the door with their family members. Outside, a ramp with a wrought-iron handrail leads down to the schoolyard. Demetrius and Pablo dart to the ramp, grab hold of the handrail, curl their legs up, and swing back and forth. I hear Demetrius say, "Aha, here comes the wolf!" Pablo echoes, "Aha, here comes the wolf!" Demetrius repeats the refrain one more time, "Aha, here comes the wolf!" In the next moment, the two boys are running down the ramp to meet their mothers.

At three years of age, the two boys connect in a moment of play that speaks volumes about their school learning. The boys reference a storybook character from a class favorite, "The Three Little Pigs." Like Hugo in Mrs. Arnold's classroom, they make a literary connection with the rhythm that shapes most days. There are stretches when things are going well, and then there are uncertainty, disruption, and unknowns—the arrival of danger. Characters like the wolf take many guises in literature and in their lives, stirring the reaction "Uh-oh, what will happen next?" The boys are heading home with this awareness in mind, the feeling of a rhythm that carries them along on a good day, and a sense that unknowns and the unexpected lie ahead.

Still in the early stages of their development, these two children share a moment in the seedbed of our greatest human potential: using their imagination to rise above immediate circumstances to see a bit of the larger picture in life, even if only for a fleeting moment. Engaging in imaginary play with someone else, and using language to do so, is something only human beings are capable of. This is where Vygotsky's and Mrs. Paley's work intersect; they both recognize the importance of providing for and cultivating imagination in play with others in school.

For forty years, Vygotsky's ideas about learning with the help of others and Vivian Paley's teaching practices have been keeping each other company in my thinking about the education of young children whose families live in poverty and those who are English-language learners. These are the children who we continue to fail in our public schools. Why are they unable to reliably get their feet on the ground in school and benefit from the education we are offering?

Vygotsky and Mrs. Paley offer new starting points for preschool and kindergarten settings that invite children's talents, potential, and long-term motivation to learn in school. Neither Vygotsky nor Mrs. Paley offer a "how-to" manual; rather, their ideas invite discussion about how schools and teachers can reach more confidently toward the high expectations set for young children's learning.

The National Academy of Education defines excellence in teaching as professionals who (1) have strong content knowledge across the curriculum areas of literature, language arts, the sciences, mathematics, social studies, and the arts; (2) understand pedagogy—methods of teaching that fit the tasks and developmental needs of students; and (3) gather ongoing knowedge about their students including monitoring and assessing progress to inform teaching (2005, 5–28). How do Vygotsky and Mrs. Paley view these three components of effective teaching at work in a Head Start classroom? After considering their comments on teaching, we will see that they offer a surprising dividend—a new vision of classroom management.

Content Knowledge: The Imagination in School

The Art Institute in downtown Chicago was built in time for the World's Columbian Exposition in 1893. It is a grand classical building with columns, arches, and two majestic lions standing guard outside its front doors. In 2009, the Art Institute opened its new Modern Wing adjoining the original museum. It is an impressive accompaniment to the original structure and yet entirely new and visionary architecturally. Renzo Piano, the renowned Italian architect who designed the building, was interviewed on the radio at the time of its opening. When asked how he came to the design for the building, knowing that it would be seen by millions of people for decades to come, he had a surprising response.

Piano said that it took him ten years to design the building, and that part of the work included just being in the city, in the area where the structure was to be built, getting a feel for the space. He said that architecture is not an art form for the moment; rather, it becomes part of the landscape, like rivers, trees, and lakes, and can be changed by events and grow with the changes that people bring to the setting, inside and out.

Piano's process of working as well as his achievement offer an analogy with early childhood education as it aims to align its goals with those of the Common Core State Standards. The standards reflect an urgency and ambitiousness that respond to current economic, social, political, and scientific challenges. We want our young children to grow up seeking out the skills and expertise of professionals who consider carefully the achievements of the past and present. We hope children will literally and figuratively build on the knowledge and practice of the physical and natural sciences, the social sciences, and the humanities. We want the talents of our children to transform their futures in ways that improve and further the well-being of others.

Children are curious, and child development theory and research confirm that they come to school with this disposition (National Research Council 2000). What if upon entering the classroom, children find teachers listening attentively for their questions and stories, demonstrating a willingness to engage them in "playing out" their ideas using classroom materials while their propensity to ask questions is at its peak? What if well-educated teachers are guiding children to observe, discuss, imagine, and debate possibilities in the company of their equally eager peers? Our youngest children could be in such conservatories of educational excellence in our public schools, preparing for their future in school and beyond. Vivian Paley affirmed this premise in a speech commemorating Lady Bird Johnson's one hundredth birthday: "We have no more important natural resource than our children. And they have no more important resource than their imaginations" (Texas State University, November 2012). Effective teaching requires imagination coupled with content knowledge—from teachers and children.

Pretend play, storytelling, and story acting in classrooms such as Mrs. Miller's and Mrs. Arnold's are providing children with space for their current and future skills to think and converse about ideas in school to flourish. With Pablo and Demetrius, we can see the imagery and words of a classic children's book working alongside and inside the flow of their daily routines. Pretend play that cultivates conversation and storytelling among friends builds the foundation for a child's imagination to move with ease beyond the immediate circumstances—now and in the decades to come.

Demetrius, Pablo, and their classmates come and go from their Head Start classroom to a neighborhood where there is no accessible health care, food shopping, or employment opportunities. They have firsthand experience with violence and trauma. In Mrs. Miller's class, several children were abused by family members and subsequently removed from their homes. One child's uncle was shot in neighborhood cross fire, and several children had family members in jail. Charleyne's aunt died at age thirty-eight from lupus, and her four children joined the young student's already-crowded household. Even with these challenging and painful circumstances to contend with, Mrs. Miller's children entered school open to making friends and learning to make creative use of the classroom's tools and activities in managing their complex lives.

As Anna Freud recognized in helping young children patch together their lives in the wake of World War II, the best therapy is a good education. Mrs. Miller's daily activities—along with the children's play, dictated stories, and story dramatizations—keep the children collectively and individually "above water," not drowning in the painful realities that burden their families and their young lives. The weaving of intellectual knowledge and skills with the inner strength the children gather from one another enable their fears, sadness, and anger to be transformed into creative sustained narratives of hope and safety. The curricular content Mrs. Miller offers from books she reads, dramatizes, and discusses enriches her students' thinking and supports them in making deeper connections between new ideas and their past experiences. Content learning for these children is about acquiring and deepening relationships among ideas in the arts, math and science, and literature—not amassing unrelated procedures and labels for the physical world around them.

Pedagogy: Teaching and Learning through Stories and Their Dramatization

Inviting Vygotsky and Mrs. Paley to guide teaching practices highlights the importance of listening to the young child's language for learning: to pretend, to approach every new experience and idea with "What if?" Pretending is what children are ready to do, and it signals the beginning of a zone of proximal development. It marks the kind of thinking now prized in the new Common Core State Standards. Harnessing the power of pretend offers some surprising adjustments in teaching and assessment practices. Thinking about time, space, the alphabet, and other children offers the opportunity to see some of the shifts that can come in early childhood classrooms.

Time. The first ingredient for in-depth thinking, where questions are raised and solutions pursued, is protecting blocks of time for children to pick an activity from among those set out by the teacher. Child-initiated activity time benefits from balance with teacher-guided small- and large-group activities. The fast-paced, changing visual stimuli of television and electronic gaming stand in stark contrast to the more contemplative mental activity that is the province of schools, where children learn to listen, create, converse, read, write, and rework ideas. Hurrying to "cover material" undermines intellectual development in young children.

Teachers recognize the gift that sustained, uninterrupted blocks of time can mean for a group of children. It is often best seen in the tears and cries of dismay when a teacher announces cleanup time after a forty- to sixty-minute period of absorption in activities in all corners of the classroom. My student teacher Melissa Archer observed her Head Start teacher pull a three-year-old child away from his play to attend to an assessment activity. The child left behind cried out, "You ruined him!" Breaking a child's concentration and flow of activity with a friend can be mentally and socially upsetting. It disregards the learning in progress. This child aptly describes the consequences of the teacher's poor timing.

It is problematic enough to have such a disruption; it may be more harmful to children who have never experienced such relationships in play in the first place. The opportunity for play with the tools of schooling, alongside the guided experiences of teachers working with small groups and gathering individual stories, is what is most at risk in today's schooling. Leaving it out will make the first rungs on the ladder of the Common Core State Standards difficult for young children in school.

With a classroom environment and schedule that allow children to interact with one another and with the artifacts of school learning, new ideas and possibilities open up for young children and teachers that they can continuously update, rework, and transform into new thinking. Besides paper, pencil, storybooks, blocks and building materials, and a doll corner, Mrs. Paley would request a roll of masking tape and floor space for the group to gather daily.

Physical space. Resa Matlock's video *Storytelling and Story Acting with Vivian Gussin Paley* (2002) portrays Mrs. Paley's visit to a preschool in Indiana, where she meets a group of four-year-olds for the first time and demonstrates storytelling and story acting over a two-day period. Mrs. Paley sets the stage using one simple action: she shows the children a roll of masking tape and then uses it to frame a square, approximately eight feet per side, on the rug in front of the group. She invites the children to take a seat on any one of the four sides of the square, leaving the center open for acting.

Mrs. Paley tells the group that she visited another preschool last week and has brought some of the children's stories with her. She reads one by a little girl named Jilly and invites the children to act it out. In doing so, she demonstrates how a teacher launches the most important space for teaching and learning: the line between our real individual lives and thinking on the stage—the shared space inside of the square. A roll of masking tape—or as Mrs. Paley describes in *Wally's Stories*, a painted seven- or eight-foot circle on the classroom floor—creates the space for zones of proximal development to come into shared focus.

What is equally important is that Mrs. Paley brings nothing else to the rug except her notebook containing the children's stories. The teaching-learning experience about to be enacted requires no props, no other materials except the children's imagination and attention. Teachers often wonder if the story-acting activity needs rehearsals, costumes, or other materials to enhance the story's production onstage. In fact, rehearsals, props, and costumes are the opposite of what this activity calls for. The more story acting relies on words, gestures, and simple improvised movements, the more effective it becomes. What matters is the group's examination of the logic and premise of an idea offered in words. This is how teachers win children's total commitment to the goals of school.

The alphabet and other materials. Do children benefit from toys that depict reality or from materials that let them create their own realities as the moment dictates? This debate in the commercial world dates to the origin of the toy industry in the late 1800s. Many Head Start and preschool classrooms today attempt to fill the shelves with animals, foods, tools, and dolls that embody every last detail of diversity and specificity that adults can imagine. Provenzano and Brett (1983) note that this is actually detrimental to young children's development; it diminishes the opportunity for them to invent and create ideas.

If a child has a bowl of wooden beads that he or she can string into patterns to make a necklace, or pretend are vegetables for soup at the doll-corner stove, or represent gold that bad guys are searching for, or use as balls rolling down a plank that children have constructed, the material is just right for the classroom. But a bowl of plastic foods—a banana, an apple, a clump of spaghetti—invites one use only: serving fruit or spaghetti when and if a child has a storyline where this will fit. The more specificity an object has, the less its value and use for children's thinking. The goal of foregrounding oral-language skills, and then written ones, can best be served in the classroom by objects that lend themselves to multiple uses, leaving it to the children to fill out the details using words.

Regarding story dictation, what is the role of pencil and paper versus computers when recording a child's story? Both tools will have benefits and constraints that can be carefully examined by teachers in their given circumstances. The story-dictation activity does not require a computer, although one could be used. My own experience has been with paper and pen.

From years of taking dictation and observing Mrs. Paley do so, I have seen how much children can learn from watching a teacher print their words on a piece of paper. When a teacher writes on a piece of paper, he or she models and the child experiences up close what it looks like to say a word and draw a configuration of symbols to represent what was just spoken. As the teacher echoes each word being written, the child can see it constructed in print conventions: "When—parrot—gets—a—shot—he—doesn't— cry. There. Your first sentence reads, 'When parrot gets a shot, he doesn't cry.' What happens next?" Children see and hear concepts of print, every mark on paper put there for a purpose. Teachers have an opportunity to talk about one sentence, or writing two more sentences before stopping, or looking for a different word. Children notice details in the writing process, because every single mark is there to record and affirm their thinking. In the early years of becoming a writer, every physical and mental detail in writing brings children closer to becoming a writer in the psychological sense— not just one who can form letters of the alphabet.

Laptops, iPads, and other digital technologies are all tools that can expand the storytelling process in the classroom. However, with preschool and children in the early primary years, it is important to keep in mind the learning opportunities at our fingertips in the dictation process. For our youngest children, learning is sensorimotor; it is physical. We want children to get their hands on pencils, paintbrushes, and markers to learn to control and manipulate these tools for representing their thinking. Printing in big letters illustrates the making of a word in a way that typing cannot. Computer technology may be appropriate in certain circumstances, but in the beginning years of schooling, there is a place for mark-making instruments in a child's hand before they take up a keyboard.

Recognizing the alphabet, letter sounds, and simple words by sight are often considered the most basic of all skills in writing and reading. Why not begin with that and make sure children have grasped these concepts before all else? Under Vygotsky and Mrs. Paley's guidance, children are immersed in the alphabet and learning of its every contour in dictation and dramatization activities. From the beginning with young toddlers and then preschoolers, basic skills involving the alphabet are mastered inside of and as a part of activities that bring children together in new, powerful, and creative ways.

In Mrs. Paley's and Mrs. Miller's classrooms, the alphabet is prominently displayed—in alphabet books, on stencils at the writing tables, on magnetic letters, and on printed cards. The children see it constantly, and, more importantly, they use it themselves. They are drawn to every twist and turn of letter shapes and sounds as their words are transcribed onto paper while dictating, and they seek their own opportunities to experiment with drawing and writing themselves.

Helping others: where stories come from. When a teacher takes dictation from a young child, other children are often nearby listening to the emerging narrative and excitedly adding to or changing the course of the storyline. The first instinct of many teachers is to say to the intruding child, "Wait, this is not your story. Let Sam tell his own. You can have your turn later." Teachers may send such a child away to another activity to prevent "interference" in a child's story.

Vygotsky and Mrs. Paley invite us to adjust our perspective, to see the other child as a valuable resource at such a moment. A child's story is never private intellectual property, completely owned and safeguarded against the influence of others. Instead, a child's thinking in school is a starting point, a beginning, that will grow stronger and more interesting when shaped and transformed with the help of others.

The operative principle for teachers to keep in mind is that the storyteller is the one who decides whether or not an idea offered should be included in an unfolding narrative. The dictation process becomes a conversation about a character or event once the child starts with an idea and the teacher writes it down. If others try to add to or edit the story, the teacher checks with the author to see whether he or she wants to accept the change. If the storyteller sticks to his or her original line of thought, the teacher can invite the child offering ideas to sign up to tell the story in the new or modified way. This creates a classroom setting where adapting ideas leads to new breakthroughs and inventions. In addition, the community grows stronger with the expanding repertoire of ideas when teachers draw attention to each new emerging strand of thinking.

In this climate, good ideas are not hoarded or hidden. Quite the opposite: they are offered to the group, and valued by the community as a chance to hear how an idea sounds in a slightly different voice. We see this process at work in the classrooms of Mrs. Miller, Mrs. Arnold, and Mrs. Jacobs, with children picking up on themes from adult-authored stories as well as ideas from classmates, where individuality and uniqueness often derive from a common set of favorite subjects. Children practice thinking and develop narratives by borrowing and expanding on ideas from one another as well as from storybooks.

When teachers invite parents or children from an older grade level to tell stories or take dictation, the classroom community expands to include strands of new thinking as different conversational partners and storytellers mediate the children's thinking. Such story partnerships have been richly portrayed in the work of Make Believe Arts under the leadership of Trisha Lee and her colleagues in London's public schools (Cremin et al. 2013).

Understanding Young Children and Assessing Their Learning

An exciting and challenging part of zones of proximal development is contending with assessment issues. What skill and knowledge can be attributed to an individual's achievement, and what belongs to the help of others?

Educators need a systematic way to gauge the individual in relation to the group he or she is currently learning with in school, and to a larger group of peers at other schools in the region or country. How can we assess learning that is happening, as Bruner describes, "in the air" among people? Watching children in the dramatization of stories exemplifies this dilemma magnificently. When children act out a story, we watch them use their imaginations to solve problems in relation to others in the moment of need. This learning does not need to be left out of our assessments and ought not be omitted if educators are to account for the full story of learning in the classroom.

When I worked with Vivian Paley, she established routines for her student teachers to carry out an activity with every child in the class such as a simple dice game, dominoes, or card games like Go Fish. Our job was to study every possible concept at work in the activity itself, to become more skilled and proficient in working with different children, and to watch which aspects of the activity a child understood or was in the process of learning. Mrs. Paley was coaching us in the science and art of teaching: know the concepts and skills reflected in the task (content knowledge), learn to carry out procedures of a task using efficient, clear methods with a wide variety of students (pedagogy), and recognize each and every child's approach, needs, and rhythms of work (child development).

Mrs. Paley taught her student teachers that every moment of teaching is simultaneously a moment of assessment. It was my job to see, hear, and note everything that was happening in a way that would contribute to a more complete picture of how the group and every individual in the class was learning and progressing. This was a daunting task, but it is exactly what good teachers are doing. I had to listen and observe closely in order to know how to intervene in a way that might further children's learning.

Later, when I studied Aleksei Leont'ev's activity theory (1981), I saw that Mrs. Paley had arrived at the same insight as Russian psychologists writing a few years earlier than herself. Leont'ev, Vygotsky's student, writes that to assess development, it is necessary to understand the task, the learner, and how the teacher situates the task in a setting and invites the child to participate, so as to make performance possible.

In 2007, Jie-Qi Chen and I wrote a book with our colleagues Ann Masur, Jennifer McCray, and Luisiana Melendez called *Bridging: Assessment for Teaching and Learning in Early Childhood Classrooms* (McNamee and Chen 2007). Our goal was to develop performance assessment activities to measure the quantitative and qualitative nature of growth and change in children's content knowledge and skills from ages three to eight. Rather than specifying what children know at age or grade level markers, we demonstrate that it is more useful to set out the touch points in conceptual development that children are likely to arrive at in individual domains of learning: English language arts, the visual arts, performing arts, sciences, and mathematics. *Bridging* selects classroom teaching and learning activities that serve two goals: the activities provide ongoing opportunities for rich learning interactions between teacher and children, and the activities are poised to provide the observant teacher with abundant data for assessing the group and each individual's progress.

We included Vivian Paley's storytelling and story-acting activities in *Bridging* because these interactions in a teacher's and child's day are saturated with information about learning that teachers can readily document if they recognize the data they have in hand. As *Bridging* activities, children's story dictations and participation in dramatization demonstrate that the early childhood profession has the kind of assessment protocols situated inside of effective teaching practice to gauge children's narrative development. Without ever having to say to the child, "Now we are going to stop everything while I test you to see how far you have come in your skill and understanding," teachers can accomplish assessment goals while they and the children are at work in daily classroom activities.

Research using *Bridging*'s assessment activities confirms what early childhood teachers already recognize: that children's emerging skills in the different domains of development are highly variable and uneven. A child's growing knowledge and skills with music or numbers might far outpace narrative skills or drawing. With young children, exposure to and experience with materials and tasks related to the wide array of disciplines that schools offer for learning vary, as do children's initial interests and talents. Early childhood education is a time for opening up these domains that subsequent schooling cultivates.

We faced a number of questions when considering performance assessment activities across the early childhood curriculum. We wanted to pick basic activities for which early childhood teachers in the full range of publicly funded schools might have the materials and resources to carry out. We adapted Nancy Smith's ground-breaking work in tracking young children's entry into painting using crayons instead of paints, because they are the one art material early childhood classrooms are likely to have. More problematic was including pretend play as a basic activity in preschool through third-grade classrooms.

We recognized that pretend play did not fit the same time and sampling parameters as the other activities presented in the book. Play itself is hard to define and pin down in a definitive set of behaviors. It is a fluid set of skills; it can be elusive and is not readily initiated by a teacher's directive, such as "draw a picture" or "read me your favorite book." In addition, pretend play as relevant to schooling involves other children. How can a teacher simply ask two, three, or even four children to play so that he or she can observe and evaluate it? Also, while socio-dramatic play is salient for children three to six years of age, games with rules become important as children begin their school-age years. How can we include such a wide range of play possibilities for three- to eight-year-olds?

After *Bridging* was published, I revisited Vivian Paley's work, and realized that, in fact, all play is not equal when it comes to schooling. There is a clear pathway to how pretend play develops when it provides value-added benefits to effective early childhood programs. Vivian Paley addresses this point in her book *A Child's Work: The Importance of Fantasy Play* (2004, 70–76). She discusses the work of Israeli educator Sara Smilansky and her 1968 study of North African immigrant children matriculating in Israeli schools without the language and past experiences in play possessed by their fellow European Jewish classmates. To address this achievement and experience gap, Smilansky worked from the premise that if children had not learned to play, then schools needed to teach the skills.

Teaching children to engage in pretend play involves working with small groups combining children with different levels of experience. The process requires the careful guidance of teachers monitoring the use of materials, helping with problem solving, and making suggestions to further develop play scenarios in words. Such an approach is nonjudgmental of a child's home background, culture, or language. It begins by recognizing that symbolic thinking and using language to tell stories are universal to children of all cultural groups. It assumes that the skills of pretend play for all children are learned and can be cultivated, and are not optional when it comes to schooling.

This brings Vygotsky's central premise that pretend play creates zones of proximal development back into the classroom. He proposes that the starting point for thinking is being able to take an object such as a block and pretend that it is something else. Likewise, young children discover they can be a dinosaur, cowboy, puppy, or princess. Once named and communicated to another, the identities and their possible storylines can be explored. The power of pretend play is that the assumptions and elaborations are happening in words, the bedrock of schooling.

Elena Bodrova and Deborah Leong (2007) advocate for Vygotsky's thinking about play in schools. They recognize the importance, and even necessity, of pretend play as a foundation for the higher-order thinking that schooling seeks to cultivate. The work of Smilansky, along with that of Bodrova and Leong, points to a scale of pretend-play skills that reflect what schooling values, and the type of play that positions children for school achievement outcomes. The scale moves from solitary play to sustained sociodramatic play with several peers over a long period of time, perhaps thirty to forty-five minutes. Their scale does not pass judgment on children's play that is solitary, nonverbal, and even moving from one area of the classroom to another. The types of children's play overlap, and children may visit many points on the continuum of play over the course of a day or week given different needs and points in thinking. The key is whether children are moving toward the upper rungs on the ladder over the years, and early childhood teachers are supporting the children's efforts to do so.

Performance assessment points out not only what children are doing but how teachers can engage and guide children toward their future. Vivian Paley describes young children when she began her career:

> Kindergartners were expected to be somewhat "babyish," and "immature" was a stage of growth, not an accusation when I began to teach. Yet compared to nursery school children, the kindergarten boys and girls had entered the graduate program in fantasy play. The themes were lengthened and deepened and their conversations were more complex and analytical. (2004, 42)

For Vygotsky and Mrs. Paley, if we deny children access to graduate studies in play, we have compromised school achievement right at the start. As educators, we contribute to the achievement gap between children of middle-class backgrounds and those who are raised in poverty when we leave children's imaginations and their cultivation of it in storytelling activities outside the classroom door.

Bridging expanded the horizon for performance assessment, documenting the process of learning as well as the children's achievements. Research shows that an important part of early childhood education that prepares children for successful learning later in the primary and elementary years is the focus on what is called executive functioning, the way children use their minds to accomplish goals in a task. In 1995, the National Education Goals panel identified four areas crucial in launching early school learning: understanding the nature of children's thinking and their knowledge base, cultivating language skills, considering social-emotional well-being, and promoting physical and motor development. At that time, this group of national experts added a fifth area: approaches to learning.

Approaches to learning are the observable qualities that children show in the process of carrying out an activity—*how* they learn. Are children playful? Chatty? Hesitant? Do they have a goal, do they engage readily, are they distracted easily? Does it take time for children to warm up to tasks? Our research team at Erikson Institute studies preschool and kindergarten children's working approaches while engaged in *Bridging* performance-assessment activities in literacy, math, science, and the visual and performing arts. While observing *what* they can achieve on the task, we also note carefully *how* they do it. In assessing how they learn, the teacher and an Erikson researcher observe each child's participation in the activity alongside peers. New aspects to zones of proximal development opened up for us, as Vivian Paley was already studying. For example, I saw a startling example of working approaches in Yvonne Bates's kindergarten classroom at Green Park Elementary School.

Learning to concentrate. It is Tuesday of the fourth week of school. Mrs. Bates is guiding her twenty-eight kindergarten children in small groups for what she calls "time for stories and words." The children work with five or six others, rotating through the following different activities during the week.

- Listening center, where children listen to an audiobook, each with their own headphones
- Letters-and-words center, where children manipulate magnetic letters to make words—their own names plus other words on index cards from current and recent class read-alouds
- Reading center, where children sit in the library area to read books
- Printing center, where children are given lined paper with each line beginning with a capital or lowercase letter; the children fill in each line, copying the letters in pencil
- Journal-writing table, where children draw a picture in their notebook, and dictate or write a word or short story to accompany it

On the day of my visit, I watch as the children go off to their assigned areas. The teacher focuses her time on assisting children working in their journals. As Ms. Bates guides a child labeling his picture of a truck with a big *T* on the page, Anderson calls out to her from the printing center, "Teacher, can I do *A*'s?"—asking whether he can write the letter *A* on his paper. Since the letter *M* is marked on their papers this day, Mrs. Bates calls back, "After you finish the

M's, Anderson. Check that the others at your table are making *M*'s too."

There is a good hum of conversation in the classroom. Children work for about fifteen minutes, and then the teacher calls for cleanup. She asks children who were working at the printing center and doing journal writing to bring their work to her. As Anderson handed her his paper, Mrs. Bates says with disappointment, "Is that all you could get done? I expected you to finish the whole page." She adds, "Maybe you were doing too much talking and not enough work." Anderson grimaces.

The group then goes off to lunch, giving Mrs. Bates time to prepare for the afternoon. She reviews the journals and papers from children who worked at the printing center. I want to talk with her about Anderson, whose paper had only five neatly printed *M*'s. I jump in, telling her that I had moved to that area of the room when I heard Anderson ask if he could "do *A*'s." I wondered whether he had something different in mind than just *M*'s. When I got there, Anderson was saying to Brandon,

> I like M! I'm a . . . I, I co-o-rate . . . con-er-ate . . . co-ter-ate . . . co-ce-trating . . . concentrating. I'm a concentrating! Watch me! I can do it! I'm going realllll slowwww.

Brandon said, "I can do that too! I do it slooooow too." Both boys had their noses almost touching the page as they drew careful straight lines for each stroke of the *M*, laboring for almost two minutes on each letter.

The two girls at the same table, however, filled their page with *M*'s in a much more carefree manner while talking about what they planned to eat for lunch today: chili, tortilla chips, apple, carrots.

"Those boys were doing exactly what you would hope for," I tell Mrs. Bates. "And Anderson had the word for it: 'concentrating'! How did he know that word?"

Mrs. Bates is taken aback. "Wow, I would have never guessed that's what was going on," she tells me. "And these *M*'s really are well formed." Mrs. Bates had talked with the children during the previous week about "concentrating" while doing careful work when she had them draw pictures of themselves with their family. She made sure to model on the easel how they were to draw with the freshly sharpened pencils, using lines to carefully represent people and their features. She said she used the word "concentrate" when asking them to be sure that every detail could be seen.

It is important to Mrs. Bates that the children learn to illustrate their thinking as carefully as she asks them to talk through their ideas and eventually write them. I tell her, "You hit a gold mine with the work of those two boys. I hope you show the whole class what they did." Since Mrs. Bates feels badly about her punitive comments to Anderson, I urge her to talk with Anderson and Brandon when they return from lunch and tell them she had made a mistake. I suggest she tell them that I heard them talk about "concentrating," and that she is proud of their careful work. She could show the class that the two boys had done just what she hoped for.

Anderson's work illustrates an essential part of setting high expectations for learning—that we care not only about *what* they are learning but also *how* they learn. Mrs. Bates knew this was important but had begun to doubt the value of the children's talk, and she acknowledged that how children approached their work often gets left by the wayside when reviewing the outcomes of learning.

Our Erikson team documented two kinds of working approaches in the one hundred preschool and kindergarten children that we studied several years ago: the evaluative, defined as behaviors that promote or hinder the child's performance; and the descriptive, interesting individual differences among children that are not necessarily related to performance. Our most significant findings concerned the variability and malleability of working approaches. First, children's working approaches vary depending on the activity. Children focus and engage in tasks differently depending on whether they involve math content, science, art, or literacy. Working approaches are not stable traits in children that are then reflected in all activities.

Second, children's working approaches change over time—they can be learned. We can teach Anderson and his classmates what it looks like to concentrate, and the children can try out the behaviors and practice them. Finally, evaluative working approaches do affect performance. How children engage in an activity, their focus, whether or not they are resourceful when they get stuck, whether they develop a plan—all of these qualities make a difference in learning and performance outcomes. This means we want to create classrooms that are like science laboratories, where there is a climate of experimentation and creative problem solving, and where conversations about how we work are as important as what we accomplish.

The work of Mrs. Bates, Mrs. Miller, and their colleagues demonstrates that teaching young children is complex work. It benefits when teachers analyze and reflect on children's work with an observing professional colleague who is invested in the teacher's success as well as the children's. One of the challenges with teaching practices in relation to the Common Core State Standards is whether we as educators are taking time to analyze, observe, and listen carefully to young children learning. Can we withhold judgment and temper our sense of urgency long enough to see children thinking, playing, and working?

Classroom Management Reimagined

Vygotsky's theory of the zone of proximal development accounts for change when everything is going well in the classroom and the focus is on learning through play and teacher-guided activities. But what about the behavior problems? What theory guides teachers when they arbitrate fights and disagreements, moments when tears flow and tempers flare? A key indicator of a teacher's effectiveness in the eyes of school administrators, parents, and children is classroom management. Helping restore balance and focus during and after an upset is one of the most important parts of a teacher's job. Teachers most often intervene saying, "Use your words!" Here, too, Vivian Paley offers a significant insight into the teacher's role in establishing the classroom as a setting to practice conflict resolution.

She discovered and learned to implement two practices through careful study of herself and children: establishing discipline without punishment in the classroom, and recognizing that no one, teacher or child, has the right to exclude another from any form of play or activity in school. Both premises about discipline in school are unique contributions to social science research and forge new ground in understanding effective teaching. Mrs. Paley models the teaching of young children in a relationship that is built on thinking through difficulties rather than keeping score of how many times a child has been bad or good.

Some twenty years into her teaching, Vivian Paley began to push further in her own thinking about the maxim "Use your words" when it came to resolving social conflict among children. She began her teaching career with the standard tools of discipline that most have accepted as rules of thumb: admonishments for the trouble-maker and a few minutes on the time-out chair as punishment. She began to rethink the latter practice as her own unhappiness grew at watching children pass time there, and as she recognized that it did not reform the behaviors that landed them in the time-out chair. She documents the beginnings of her uneasiness in *Wally's Stories* (1981), develops new insights in *Mollie Is Three: Growing Up in School* (1986), and then finally turns the tables on punishment and time-out in *The Boy Who Would Be a Helicopter* (1990) and *You Can't Say You Can't Play* (1992).

Mrs. Paley realized that the time-out chair is equivalent to send-ing a child to jail for actions and words that they have not under-stood yet, and that are the responsibility of educators to teach in school. When using the time-out chair, teachers disregard their number one responsibility: to teach.

Mrs. Paley then wrestled with the question of how the teacher could use fair and inclusive principles to resolve classroom conflict without punishment. She found it in a new discipline, a strict pol-icy enforced by children and their teachers: no one has the right to exclude another from any activity for any reason. That is, "You can't say you can't play."

What options does a teacher have besides removing a child from a troubled scene? He or she joins the children and make it clear that no one is allowed to hurt others, themselves, or to disrupt the activi-ties under way. The teacher then finds a resolution with the children.

The final outcome of the troubled situation is not his or hers alone to decide. The outcome lies in the power of words and reasoning, which the teacher has the important responsibility to model, guide, and demonstrate in every detail. Most teachers initially respond, "I can't stop and reason with children every time there is disorder!" The task of teaching fair and inclusive practices seems too much to bring to the table when the steep agenda of learning goals awaits classroom teachers at the start of each school day.

As currently conceived, learning standards create a divide between social-emotional learning goals and intellectual outcomes. They suggest that teachers must attend to learning in separate domains: "hard" learning outcomes that are evident in test scores, and "soft" outcomes that are evident within the classroom. In the work of Vygotsky and Mrs. Paley, we see no such dichotomy, and achieving 21st Century Skills depends on the integration of the two. Dramatization offers a vision of how both sets of goals can be reconciled in teaching and learning. In dramatizing stories from the full breadth of disciplines, Vivian Paley offers a curriculum for studying both the intellectual and social interaction aspects of classroom learning with a large group of children.

Mrs. Paley offers early childhood educators a fresh perspective on disruptive, challenging behavior: it represents poor acting, a piece of bad staging, a scene that needs replaying, reworking, revisiting. Her commitment to acting out stories gave her an important insight about another aspect of teaching: classroom management.

> Well into my teaching career, I learned that good and bad play are usually a matter of having a script that works or one that needs to be rewritten. Once you begin to depend on storytelling and story acting, you start looking at your classrooms as theater. The children are constantly imagining characters and plots and, when they have a chance, with each other, acting out little stories. You can look at the children and yourself as actors. "Well, this hasn't worked. We'd better think of a better way to pretend this story." What seems to be a chaotic scene, one we might call bad play, is simply a scene that lacks closure for one or more characters.

The teacher's role is to help the children make up a new scene. The children become used to the teachers—or even other children— saying, "This isn't working. We need to tell the story of what we're doing with each other. What characters are we playing? And what needs to be played in a different way so that the play does not have to stop?" (Meghan Dombrick-Green interview with Vivian Paley 2001)

Dramatization recognizes that teachers are teaching not a single child but in fact a large group of twenty-four to thirty-five children, individually and as a group. Regulation of emotions and behavior needs guidance from the community as well as a commitment from each individual. Mrs. Paley achieved this through dramatization. In this activity structure, each child's needs and challenges are everyone else's business to consider, accommodate, and include with respect and creativity. Children learn that they are responsible for the code of fairness and inclusion right along with the teacher.

In classrooms without punishment, there is strict discipline. The teacher's control is providing a consistent authoritative approach to acceptable behaviors—as in the staging of stories on stage or screen. Clear and strict lines are drawn to ensure safety and kindness, and to stop behaviors that harm others, oneself, or classroom materials. The teacher becomes the leader and model for using words to solve problems and restore fairness. Mrs. Paley's writings, as Patricia Cooper explains, offer a "pedagogy of fairness" that fits the premises of zones of proximal development—giving and receiving help with others who are friends in learning (2009, 93–105).

Everyday restlessness. Even on good days in the classroom, my student teachers can become discouraged with what can seem like inattentiveness during teacher-directed group activities—for example, during the dramatization of stories. Children's squirming, wanting a turn in every story, or daydreaming while stories are being acted out convince novice teachers that they are losing control of the group, or make them question whether they had it to begin with. They prefer not to pursue an activity that exposes their fears about control in the classroom.

Every teacher wonders about children's restlessness at some

level: "How much disruption, talking, inattentiveness do I take for granted or accept as part of the classroom climate? When do I rein in a child or the group and set higher expectations for focus and participation?" Many factors must be considered in answering these questions on a given day.

Being in a classroom with twenty or more children at ages three to six years for a half or even a full day is a strain, and an unnatural idea when we think about it from a young child's point of view. Children's needs are often left by the wayside for the sake of adult goals and notions of convenience. Complying with classroom protocols requires a huge adjustment on the part of young children; some days they handle it better than others.

I learned from Mrs. Paley to observe the restlessness, and then look beyond it. When I was a student teacher in her classroom, Mrs. Paley had twenty-four students as well as two assistant teachers. I remember days when children rolled around on the rug, chatted with others near them, or crawled under a table. I saw Mrs. Paley watching it all, keeping a close eye on everything while continuing on with her lesson most of the time. If the commotion did not bother other children, Mrs. Paley was comfortable letting much of it go without comment. She did not demand or expect perfection.

I recently wrote a letter to Mrs. Paley about my memory of her acceptance of everyday restlessness in young children as it relates to leading discussions with children. She replied with her own thoughts about what had been happening.

> I've been thinking about your feeling that I did not worry about children being distracted during a discussion, that I trusted the children to stick to the subject if I continued to stick with the subject myself, and avoided becoming distracted by their behaviors. I think I was learning to do something else as well. I wanted my behavior to set an example of polite respectful conversation, the sort that does not keep pointing out people's failures to them and to others.
>
> Your students need not be concerned. They will get the hang of it, and their children will see that their teachers are simply trying to have good conversations in which everyone's ideas can shine through. Let

me ask a question: When your students transcribe a discussion for you and for their classmates, can they "edit out" the disciplinary warnings to some extent? Or is the final form, as written, supposed to contain all the bones and tissues?

... If a writer grows accustomed to editing out distractions, there may be a good self-teaching aspect to this notion. The habit of self-editing may help your students actually see more clearly themselves where the real story lies in a discussion. In other words, the student teacher keeps asking herself, "Where is the story in this discussion?" and becomes less interested in physical behaviors.

Let me see, how would this work? Instead of "Tommy, come back to your place!" the teacher might say, "John, could you say that again, about what Batman was doing? I wasn't listening closely enough. Tell us again exactly what he said to the bad guys."

You see, everyone knows why I wasn't able to listen closely. The point is made easily. (Personal communication, December 18, 2013)

Observing Mrs. Paley was very important during my apprenticeship because I thought an expert teacher had no behavior issues. This is not true. I learned from her to aim high, expect progress in the direction I wanted the group to go in, pay close attention to everything, and end group times graciously, like Mr. Gumpy, the hero of John Burningham's story *Mr. Gumpy's Outing* (1970).

Mr. Gumpy is an English farmer preparing to go out rowing on a river. Different farm animals come along through the fields asking if they can come too: a goat, a calf, chickens, a pig, and sheep. Mr. Gumpy welcomes them, as well as some children, into the boat but asks them kindly not to tease, trample, kick, or muck about. Before long, his passengers begin to do exactly that; the boat tips over, and everyone falls into the water. They swim ashore, dry off, and go back to his house for tea with a spread of sandwiches and cakes. The group looks elegant and well disciplined sitting around his huge table. He invites them all to "come again another day."

Mr. Gumpy models a teacher's steady vision and guidance pursuing civilized behavior in the classroom with plenty of learning along the way. Teachers are responsible for showing what an inclusive, caring community looks like, expressing confidence in the goal, and articulating how to make it work. Enacting stories and replaying difficult moments in dramatizations are the key tools that Vivian Paley models for helping teachers lead such classrooms. Vygotsky is nodding in agreement.

Chapter 9

Teaching Friends

"The stone which the builders rejected has now become the cornerstone."
VIVIAN PALEY, *The Boy on the Beach: Building Community through Play*

"The stone that the builders have disdained must become the foundation
stone." LEV VYGOTSKY, *Problems of General Psychology*

Both Mrs. Paley and Vygotsky refer to this Bible passage (Psalm
118:22) in their writings. These references do not seek a religious
or spiritual interpretation. From different vantage points, both Vygotsky and Mrs. Paley propose a major shift in how we think about
children and their development. Both offer views of children un-
likely to be recognized at first glance by the "builders" in education or psychology. Their unique insights into how learning among
young children works in school are worth considering carefully.

Consider the literal image of the Bible verse: when working
thousands of years ago, stonecutters carefully examined each stone
before selecting one for a building they were constructing. The ones
that did not conform to their specifications were discarded. Vygotsky
and Mrs. Paley both reference this passage to remind us to pause for
a moment before we move on. What might seem unusable at first
glance may become what another artist, builder, and, in our case,
child and educator use as the starting point for something new.

Vygotsky and Mrs. Paley offer starting points for a new vision
of public education. Both suggest that when young children play
and learn, they consider all kinds of ideas that are offered to them.
When ideas are offered within enacted scenes, children see with
deeper clarity and purpose. They pick up on ideas that we might
least expect as interesting or significant and consider them as a basis
for a new line of thinking, a hypothesis. When ideas are offered in

the context of storytelling and story acting, children discover that ideas are cornerstones for new ideas where nothing has to be set in stone. In daily storytelling, ideas remain fluid and malleable while teachers learn how to be present and listen with an ear to the children's past and future. Children can study how ideas form over a period of years—like architect Renzo Piano's preparation for the Art Institute's new wing.

The dramatization of children's dictated stories as well as stories from literature opens the way for Head Start children to actively participate in building their thinking and their future, with schools and teachers as partners and coaches. It takes a pad of paper, pencil, a wealth of interesting literature, and a well-educated teacher who listens to individuals and makes connections for the group when the class comes together to enact ideas at the center of everyone's thinking—the teacher's and the children's.

The work of Vygotsky and Mrs. Paley invite us to consider standards for teaching and learning that privilege the imagination as set in motion *among* a group of children. The two seek what Jerome Bruner would describe as an intelligence in the air among the participants in a classroom that sustains the group and that makes possible the achievement of all (1962). For them, success is measured by the progress of the whole: the most vulnerable and the most talented in a thoughtful and resourceful community.

The work of future educators is to understand how to operationalize this standard if we hope to close the achievement gap. Studying dramatization of ideas has brought me closer to this responsibility as an educator than any other single teaching experience. Vygotsky and Mrs. Paley teach us that assembling children in a group and presenting lessons does not make a community. Community for teachers means utilizing the human need to belong, to be a part of a group—be it family, peers, or classroom—in supporting everyone's next step forward in learning. Community means recognizing the interdependence of participants; children want and depend on one another's help in growing up. Dramatizing ideas provides the necessary structure for such a learning community, as it requires words to portray and examine ideas under the teacher's direction. Dramatizing stories provides the unique opportunity for children to show one another and their teacher what their thinking looks like, and to serve as one another's lifeline in their next steps growing up in school.

First Day in Kindergarten

The children in Mrs. Miller's class attend Head Start in a public school, but they will not necessarily attend kindergarten there. Different geographical boundaries determine preschool versus elementary-school assignments. Mrs. Miller's children will not take their next step forward in school together; their friendships and stories will go their separate ways as five-year-olds.

In January of the school year, I visited a kindergarten classroom in a school near Green Park to begin a professional development relationship with Cynthia James, six months before she might meet one of Mrs. Miller's students. She invited me to observe and interact with her children when I had time.

The morning of my first visit, school is already well under way. Mrs. James is busy at a table with a small group of children leading a phonics lesson. It is "center time" for the other twenty-three children. One group sits at a table playing a game; others are making puzzles and reading books in the library area. On the rug, three children are playing with blocks, but things are not going well.

As I approach, a little boy sits on his knees with big tears rolling down his cheeks. Two girls are grabbing up blocks. When I ask what he wants to build, he stares at me and pulls a tub of dinosaurs closer. But when I ask if he wants to tell me a story before he starts to build and offer to write it down, his eyes brighten. He has never seen me before, I have never been in the classroom, do not know his teacher, and out of the blue I appear and ask him if he wants to tell a story. The request makes sense to him.

I tell the child to go ahead and tell me his story. He watches my every movement with the pen and dictates in perfect rhythm to my writing. His storyline is as clear as a bell and comes without hesitation.

Once upon a time, I was riding a motorcycle. A dragon came and attacked me. And then I put him up in a cage and bring him to the jungle.

He then starts building a castle with blocks alongside the two girls. They make a long line of blocks stacked two and three high as a castle wall. The three of them "lived happily ever after" until cleanup time. The boy was on a better footing to participate in play almost immediately after collecting his thoughts to tell a story.

While the boy and two girls are building, another child, the boy's cousin, is completing a worksheet at a table. He comes to ask my help with it, wondering if he needs to put an *X* on the two pictures he is considering. The worksheet presents two columns with a pair of pictures in each column. There are a total of six pictures in each column to compare. The instructions ask the child to circle the pair of pictures if the middle sound in the pair of words is the same, and strike with an *X* those that are not the same. The words do not necessarily rhyme. He has completed column one and is halfway down column two. The pair he is stuck on is "bed, net." He asks me which word goes with the picture of the net.

We work through the rest of the sheet together, him saying the words that he thinks go with the picture, and me supplying the correct word if need be, repeating the word pair ("pig, pot"; "sun, cut") to see if he can distinguish the sounds.

The task is a struggle for a five-year-old who is not familiar with some of the graphics presented and may use different words for the objects presented. In addition, the pronunciation of words and vowels sound different in his home dialect.

When he is done, this child puts his paper in a bin and returns to the rug. He had seen me writing his cousin's story on my notebook page and asks me to write "the." After I do so, he smiles to see it. I tell him that if he has a story to tell, I will write it down, and I read his cousin's story to him. He is pleased with the invitation and, without hesitating, says,

A dragon helped me and the princess came to save me.

We act out both stories right there amid the blocks with the four children.

As teachers we are both dragon and princess (or prince) in the children's lives, and so too are the children to one another. It takes all kinds of friendships in school to make learning possible, and the days when we bring new stories to one another are good ones. The simplest of words—"Do you have a story to tell?"—awakens a zone of proximal development for teacher and child, and among the children themselves.

Within a few short minutes, four children and I are in relationships that can build and grow from nothing to story. Very quickly, there is purpose to creating a shared narrative and a mutual vested interest in one another's goals. Everyone's well-being is implicated in each child's success, and each child's success is needed for the strength of all. Literacy success is achievable if we understand how to build and sustain thriving communities in which enacting stories is the cornerstone.

Last Day in Head Start

The last day of school for Mrs. Miller, Mrs. Ortiz, and their Head Start students is a red-letter day. The Green Park Elementary classroom is a flurry of activity, from the block area to the doll corner, water table, and art table. Stories ebb and flow around the urgencies of daily tensions and anticipation of ending the school year.

Eighteen children are in school. Eight signed up to tell a story first thing in the morning, and by the end of the morning, ten children have dictated stories, with three more children eager to tell one. They will have to wait until kindergarten for their next opportunity—if it is offered.

Mrs. Miller calls for cleanup forty minutes before the end of the day. She and I compare notes: there is a long list of stories to act out, and the room is a mess. Heavy layers of paper scraps litter the floor around the art table. Every block is being used on the rug. The doll corner is scattered with dishes, doll babies, and their clothes. The disarray is a tribute to the rich whirl of activity that now needs to come to a focus. Mrs. Miller, Mrs. Ortiz, and I work inch by inch around the room to help children put away materials one last time. Charleyne and Lawrence do not want to put down their brooms and continue to circle the art table for a few minutes, brushing the clean floor.

The children on the rug are wiggly and excited. I start singing the

Russian folk song "May There Always Be Sunshine," and the children join in. We add a second verse: "May there always be babies, may there always be friends, may there always be dinosaurs, may there always be school." Carlos shouts out, "Dads!" More wishes follow: apples, birthdays, Batman . . . their requests foreshadow the stories to come.

I start with the reminder that we will go around the circle, giving everyone a turn to act out a part. Each child and their beloved characters come on stage one last time, as one story follows another.

The first story is Chantell's. She had dictated her story as soon as she came into the classroom and put away her backpack. She introduced a new princess image to the girls' fantasy characters, Tinker Bell. She also added to the growing imagery of the season's happiest ball, a quinceañera, which Daniella had introduced a week earlier in her story about fifteen princesses.

> Once upon a time, there was a green Tinkerbell. There was a blue Tinkerbell and a lot of Tinkerbell babies. I had a quinceañera, and all three of the princesses. And then I'm going to the quinceañera and I go buy my mama a dress. I rock my baby to sleep. And I go in the kitchen and make my baby some food. And some dinosaurs eat the princesses. I cut the princesses out of the dinosaur's tummy. And then the princesses go home and be alone. The end.

When Chantell came to the word *quinceañera*, I paused and showed her how I had to page back in my notebook to Daniella's story of the previous week to be sure of the correct spelling of the word. I told her, "I checked the dictionary when I got home last week to see how this word is spelled. Look how long that word is!" She watched me as I wrote it down with the tilde over the *n*. When she finished dictating her story, I asked her how the princesses got home if the dinosaurs had eaten them. She then added the sentence, "I cut the princesses out of the dinosaur's tummy."

Charleyne had her own version of the girls' celebratory night out.

> It's a princess in a lovely dress. And then she had some lovely friends. Then they had a dance together and they each had to call somebody.

And they had fun. Then they like to go play with a priddle, texting her friends. They do a dance by their selves. Her like to play with their friends and they go to a club. They dance. They like to play together and they dancing.

When Charleyne was dictating her story and came to the word *priddle*, we all heard it: Chantell, Juan, Daniella, and Anthony. When I asked her what a priddle was, Charleyne replied, "You know, a priddle." I then asked her to act it out. She sort of danced around and moved her fingers. I asked the others around us what the word meant. I reread the story. No one knew what she was trying to say. We thought it was some sort of game or new dance movement. So I left it as she said it and told her that she could act this out for the group.

When we act out the story, I tell the group that Charleyne's story has a word, *priddle*, and that none of us knew what it meant but she would act it out for us it. Mrs. Miller repeats the word. "Priddle? Hmmm." Then Charleyne points to the computers. Mrs. Miller says, "'Puter? Computer?!" "Yeah!" shouts Charleyne, with a huge smile. The sentence now made sense. She had been conflating the words *computer* and *cell phone*. It is a wonderful moment of clarity for Charleyne and the attentive group. During dictation, we were stuck without a way to reach across a gulf of word sound and its meaning, but at least we knew exactly where the problem was: one word in one scene. The day feels more complete now that this word has a shared meaning that we can act out.

Earlier in the day, when Charleyne is dictating her story, Juan is trying to staple Popsicle sticks together. I tell him not to—that he will break the stapler. He insists he can do it. I want to push ahead with Charleyne's story dictation, but I also worry he will break the stapler or cut his finger on a sharp staple. I am annoyed that he will not listen to me but decide to let it go and keep a close eye on his work. Juan is angry today. He doesn't like his new haircut—a closely shaved buzz cut. I finish Charleyne's story and then turn back to Juan, who is now using two sticks to fashion a winged plane. He leaves the table and returns with a pipe cleaner. I tell him he has a great idea and offer to hold the sticks while he uses the pipe cleaner to fasten them together. He twists the pipe cleaner around the two sticks; when he is done, they stay in place. I am thrilled with his success, but he is not. He flies his new "plane" right in front of my face, then Charleyne's, then over my right hand, finally flying it under the table at Charleyne's feet. I reach down, pick it up, and hand it back to him.

Finally, I ask Juan if he has an airplane story to tell. He nods and dictates quietly.

The airplane cut my hair [meaning it flew so close to our foreheads, it cut our hair!] and shoot me. The airplane flies.

I realize that through his story he is revisiting the experience of getting his hair cut. I suggest he put the airplane he made in his cubby and that when we act it out later, he bring it to the rug. (Later, he acted the story out happily—without the airplane.)

I move on to the table of small toys where Carlos, Pablo, Lawrence, and Demetrius are using waffle blocks to build small square houses for their animal figurines. The table is full of stories about the animals. I know several of these boys are on the story list, and I think this would be a good opportunity to draw them out. They are ready—but to my surprise, none of the stories relate to the animals.

Carlos goes first. I had asked him earlier if he would tell a Batman story today. He said no then, but now the superhero is the star of his story.

Batman and Robin come but there was two Batmans. Robin didn't know which one was Batman. He didn't figure it out. Robin is trying to think which one it was. And then Batman talked and he knew which one was Batman. Batman was the one who talked and said, "I'm Batman." Then there was a big monster chameleon. He broke the boat and the boat was his door. He slammed the boat and went through the water. The end.

Carlos is using waffle blocks to illustrate the boat. Demetrius wants to tell a story next. I ask Carlos if he will stay nearby to help me translate any words I am not sure of. He agrees and continues playing with the little animals.

Demetrius is very excited about Batman scenarios but cannot get the storyline quite right in the beginning: "Batman, he don't like Joker. No, Batwoman don't like Joker."

I reread the sentence and ask, "Does Batwoman like or not like Joker?" Then Carlos jumps in and corrects him, "Batman *likes* Joker." Demetrius clarifies, "Batwoman likes Joker."

Carlos jumps in and adds, "Because he's invisible; he's from outer space." I ask Demetrius, "Do you want that part in your story?" He nods his head excitedly so I write it down word for word. Demetrius continues, using gun sound effects to describe Batman shooting. "He go in the house and go in the house again. Batwoman, he like a house. Batman like Joker."

With Vygotsky in mind, I realize I am watching a slightly older and more capable student help his younger classmate grow in his narrative skills. The boys joined forces in friendship around Batman, with the younger child happily reaching for the narrative clarity of his heroes: Batman and Carlos.

I invite Pablo, whose English vocabulary is also limited, to tell his story since Carlos is still nearby to translate. Carlos's love of stories and ready interest in helping others give him an important role to play. In a tentative, tiny voice, Pablo starts in on his story.

"A car was bigger and bigger," he says.

Carlos jumps in again: "He transformed to a car and a fire truck, right?"

Pablo nods happily and continues,

And four dinosaurs! And a dog was fighting with a fire truck and a dog fell. And a bear was fighting with a dog and the bear was dead. Three dinosaurs, there are a lot of dinosaurs. The end.

With that, the boys pick up the waffle blocks and go back to building houses for the sheep and cows.

Daniella is next on the list. She and Chantell are in the doll corner squabbling over baby clothes. Chantell does not want Daniella to hold any baby dolls, and Daniella complains that Chantell wants all the clothes. Chantell says that she is hungry and wants to cook. She had eaten lunch but I sense she is hungry for something besides food.

She suddenly says, "Do you want me to cook food? You can take care of the babies." She frees herself and Daniella from the impasse.

The girls gather up the babies, and Chantell passes hers off to Daniella. Daniella sits in a rocking chair holding them while Chantell begins to cook. Chantell says forcefully, "Dress them!" I ask Daniella if she wants to dictate her story while dressing the doll babies. She says yes, ready with her favorite themes of princesses going to the ball, taking care of babies, and getting married. And yet on this last day, she offers a cast of characters that are new to this classroom community.

> Once upon a time there was Beauty and the Beast. There was a birthday ball and the Lady-in-Waiting did not like it. The Lady-in-Waiting slap Robin Hood. Robin Hood let the princess go off to the ball. The Lady-in-Waiting is her mother and she find out. Robin Hood went to the princess's window and knocked on the door. Then the princess and Robin Hood went off to the ball and got married. Robin Hood ate the Lady-in-Waiting. The princess had a baby and fix the baby some food. Then they get married again.

Chantell piles the table beside Daniella with food that she announces as she delivers it: ice cream, broccoli, hot dogs, pizza, dinner rolls, and mashed potatoes. The doll corner has found its balance with the cooking and storytelling. The babies are back in good care.

I stop by the block area, where Miguel is playing with the plastic dinosaurs. When I ask if he is ready with a story, he says yes. Carlos looks up from his play with the miniature animals and once again eagerly volunteers to help. Miguel had not told a story since the March day in the hallway when Carlos offered his Batman story to Miguel. Miguel dictated three stories this year, and Carlos was present for all of them. Miguel starts in, Carlos listening but never saying a word.

> My story is about McQueen. McQueen was going to find his friend. But then he couldn't find him. Then a giant car went to him. And then McQueen say, "Help!" And then a dinosaur went to help him. And McQueen went away with the dinosaur and was his friend.

As I write, echoing each word aloud, I recognize that this story is the perfect expression of friendship: Miguel recognizing Carlos's gesture of friendship and willingly receiving it. In his story, Miguel is McQueen, a character out in the world in search of a friend. A dinosaur, a character of large proportions, hears his call for help and they become friends. Miguel is moving forward in life with Carlos opening the way to learning for him with knowledge and confidence, bringing an ease to the helping process that few teachers can match. Miguel thrives in the zones of proximal development that he finds in this classroom, with Carlos as one of his teachers.

Anthony sits quietly building one of his elaborate structures with blocks. Edythe, who hardly ever speaks in school, sits silently beside him, handing him blocks, absorbed in watching him place each one. It is a rare moment of interaction between two of the quietest children in the classroom.

Anthony speaks with his hands every day, and the class recognizes and admires his visual artistic skill. Over lunch, Mrs. Miller points out the butterflies Anthony had invented, using figure-eight-shaped strips of paper, and taught the class to make over the past two days as they read and acted out *The Chick and the Duckling* (Ginsburg 1972). Mrs. Miller helped attach yarn to the butterflies and then hung them from the ceiling of the classroom. A cluster of butterflies surround Chantell's and Maria's drawings of a duck and a chick, which Anthony had cut out with his steady hand so they too could be hung up with the butterflies.

Anthony had not signed up for story dictation, but after Edythe goes to the washroom, I ask him if he would like to tell a story. He nods yes eagerly. He moves closer to the notebook to watch me write each word he says.

> Batman take the treasure. Batman open the treasure and get the
> money. Batman shared the treasure with Robin. Batman said, "Take
> the treasure and there won't be anymore."

Carlos is still playing with dinosaurs across the rug. I see him look up when Anthony mentions Batman. Carlos listens a moment and then returns to his play with Miguel. This is a finely tuned community, sensitive to story content in dictation and play. Both Carlos and Anthony offer a great deal to other children, one verbally and one visually, but giving nonetheless.

Edythe tells the last story. She is a thin, tiny child who moves around the classroom like a shadow, rarely talking. I hadn't noticed her return from the washroom, but when the students are given the five-minute warning before cleanup, she taps me on the shoulder and whispers, "I have a story." I say, "Great, there's just enough time."

Edythe told four stories during the school year: one in December, one in January, one in April, and now on the last day. Her first story had been mostly a list of characters, a series of nouns with a few verbs surfacing toward the end.

> A baby girl. A baby mommy. A daddy, baby mama, baby son, baby daughter, baby walking stick, baby stroller, the baby sleep. Daughter wake. Daughter sleeping. Daughter wake. Mama wake.

Her story seems to be saying, "In the beginning, there were mommies and babies. Even the mommies were once a baby. Life in the beginning is sleeping and waking."

Today's story has a full-blown plot. Her opening line shocks me. Her narrative seems to jump right into the present, as fully developed as those told by other four-year-olds.

> A princess grab the monster's neck. The monster run away and locks the door. The princess run away and the monster come back to the girl's house. And the girl said, "Get out!" [Edythe says this more loudly than anything we had heard from her this year.] The princess run away in the mama's house. The monster grabs the grandma's house and throw it on the grandpa's house. The monster run away and go into the grandpa's house.

Edythe has been listening and quietly working things out in her own mind, observing everything and everyone. This tiny wisp of a girl who rarely speaks provides the grand finale to the school year.

Edythe's story is a tale of a princess and a monster who both dare to speak out and act in bold, defiant ways. They both set clear boundaries and seek safety in a grandparent's house. Edythe, like several of her classmates, has a number of unbearable hardships to navigate in her young life. And yet for her, as with all children, the language of learning in school is in the invitation to transform her ideas into a story that can be shared in dramatizations with her classmates. Her teachers asked, "What story do you have to tell? How does it go? Let's see what it looks like when we act it out." When storytelling and story acting are part of the curriculum, children listen to what others have to say and offer new images to the community—a literary one.

The last day of storytelling for these children celebrated the characters that they cared for and protected day after day, binding this literary community in their first school experience: dinosaurs, dragons, Batman, princesses, and their babies. Some characters were unique, like Blue Tinker Bell, and yet were cast in familiar and recognizable plots. Equally recognizable were the offers of friendship that authors extended to one another—and that the three teachers could support and facilitate when we were tuned into community dynamics.

Over the course of the twenty-four days that I visited Mrs. Miller's Head Start classroom during the school year, the children told 120 stories—an average of five stories dictated and acted out each day. Exactly half were told by English-language learners, attesting to the power of inclusion these activities offered. Every child in the class told at least one story, and all of the children had a part in the story acting every day. On some days the stories flowed; other times, a mere trickle of dictations emerged from the day's activities. Although the children's stories ebbed and flowed among the other classroom activities and daily read-alouds, the teachers were interested and committed to listening and ensuring the children's voices were heard. Dramatization helped the children connect their thinking with others and reflect on new possibilities for the next school day. Within this structure, both the teachers and a classroom of storytellers grew individually and together: the children changed and progressed within the zone of proximal development of the class.

In assessing the children's progress over the school year, we can count the number of stories each child told, the number of words they used, the complexity of their grammatical sentences, and the stages of narrative development they achieved. However, every classroom teacher knows that such tallies overlook the growth in the classroom community. The most enduring and powerful achievements are in the friendships formed among children and with their teachers, all of whom were listening to one another. Edythe's change over time was influenced by Daniella, by the other children, and by her teachers. Edythe's learning came from the collective of teaching friends. "The strength of the pack is the wolf," wrote Rudyard Kipling in *The Jungle Book* (1894). "The strength of the wolf is the pack."

Mrs. Miller's leadership in dramatizing stories enabled Daniella, Edythe, Carlos, Demetrius, Lawrence, and their classmates to contribute to the achievement of all children, especially the most vulnerable. Therein lies the power of storytelling and story acting as the zone of proximal development par excellence in school— success for all.

The children sit around their snack tables eating fruit and crackers during their last five minutes of Head Start together. I pull up a chair next to Carlos and Edythe. Edythe whispers, "I have another story to tell." I tell her I know she had lots more, and that I hope she will keep telling her stories in kindergarten. I swallow the disappointment that there is no time left to hear one more story. I fear that Edythe may go for years without another teacher asking her what story she has to tell. I gulp back sadness that these children will not see Mrs. Miller and Mrs. Ortiz, their classroom, this school, or one another as a group again. They will disperse to enroll in designated "neighborhood schools."

After a pause, Carlos looks up from his orange slice and says with confidence, "I want to grow up and be a teacher." Vygotsky and Mrs. Paley hope that he does. He is a bellwether of standards for learning, teaching, and friendship with young children in their earliest years of schooling.

References

Bettelheim, Bruno. 1982. *The empty fortress: Infantile autism and the birth of the self.* New York: The Free Press.

Bodrova, Elena, and Deborah Leong. 2007. *Tools of the mind: The Vygotskian approach to early childhood education.* Upper Saddle Hill, NJ: Pearson Education, Inc.

Brazelton, T. Berry, and Joshua Sparrow. 2006. *Touchpoints: Birth to three.* Cambridge, MA: Perseus Publishing.

Bruner, Jerome. 1962. Introduction to *Thought and language,* by L. S. Vygotsky, v–x. Cambridge, MA: MIT Press.

———. 1966. "On cognitive growth I." Pp. 1–29 in *Studies in cognitive growth,* edited by Jerome Bruner, Rose Olver, and Patricia Greenfield et al. New York: Wiley.

———. 1983. *Child's talk: Learning to use language.* New York: W. W. Norton and Company.

———. 1986. *Actual minds, possible worlds.* Cambridge, MA: Harvard University Press.

Cazden, Courtney. 2001. *Classroom discourse: The language of teaching and learning.* Portsmouth, NH: Heinemann.

Chen, Jie-Qi, and Gillian McNamee, with Ann Masur, Jennifer McCray, and Luisiana Melendez. 2007. *Bridging: Assessment for teaching and learning in pre-k to 3 classrooms.* Thousand Oaks, CA: Corwin Press.

Cole, Michael. 1996. *Cultural psychology: A once and future discipline.* Cambridge, MA: Belknap / Harvard Press.

Cole, Michael, and Peg Griffin. 1986. "A sociohistorical approach to remediation." Pp. 110–31 in *Literacy, society, and schooling,* edited by Suzanne DeCastell, Allan Luke, and Kieran Egan. New York: Cambridge University Press.

Cooper, Patricia. 1993. *When stories come to school: Telling, writing and performing stories in the early childhood classroom.* New York: Teachers and Writers Collaborative.

———. 2009. *The classrooms all young children need: Lessons in teaching from Vivian Paley.* Chicago: University of Chicago Press.

Cremin, Teresa, Joan Swann, Rosie Flewitt, Dorothy Faulkner, and Natalia Kucirkova. 2013. *Evaluation report of MakeBelieve Arts Helicopter Technique of storytelling and story acting.* London: Open University.

Delpit, Lisa. 1995. *Other people's children: Cultural conflict in the classroom.* New York: The New Press.

Dombrink-Green, Meghan. 2001. "A conversation with Vivian Gussin Paley." *Young children* (September). http:// http://www.naeyc.org/content/conversation-vivian-gussin-paley.

Fountas, Irene, and Gay Su Pinnell. 1996. *Guided reading, good teaching for all children.* Portsmouth, NH: Heinemann.

Green, Connie. 2009. *The Lydia year: Learning from pre-kindergarten children in rural Appalachia.* New York: Association for Childhood Education International.

Griffin, Peg, and Michael Cole. 1984. "Current activity for the future: The zo-ped." Pp. 45–64 in *New directions for child development*, no. 23, edited by B. Rogoff and James V. Wertsch. San Francisco: Jossey-Bass.

Jackson, Phil, with Hugh Delehanty. 2006. *Sacred hoops: Spiritual lessons of a hardwood warrior.* New York: Hyperion.

Kagan, Sharon Lynn, E. Moore, and Susan Bredekamp, eds. 1995. *Reconsidering children's early development and learning: Toward common views and vocabulary* (Goal 1 Technical Planning Group, reprint no. 95-03). Washington DC: National Education Goals Panel.

Katch, Jane. 2001. *Under deadman's skin: Discovering the meaning of children's violent play.* Boston: Beacon Press.

———. 2003. *They don't like me.* Boston: Beacon Press.

Kipling, Rudyard. 1894. *The jungle book.*

Labov, William. 1972. "The logic of nonstandard English." Pp. 225–61 in *Language and cultural diversity in American education,* edited by Roger Abrahams and Rudolph Troike. Englewood Cliffs, NJ: Prentice-Hall.

Leont'ev, Aleksei N. 1981. "The problem of activity in psychology." Pp. 39–71 in *The concept of activity in Soviet psychology,* edited by James V. Wertsch. Armonk, NY: M.E. Sharpe.

Lindfors, Judith. 1987. *Children's language and learning.* Englewood Cliffs, NJ: Prentice-Hall.

Matlock, Resa. *Storytelling and story acting with Vivian Gussin Paley.* 2002. Muncie, IN: The Child Care Collection at Ball State University, DVD.

Matlock, Resa, and Randy Testa. 2001. *A companion booklet to the video "The boy who could tell stories" by Vivian Gussin Paley.* Muncie, IN: The Indiana Center on Early Childhood Development, Ball State University.

McLane, Joan, and Gillian McNamee. 1990. *Early literacy*. Cambridge, MA: Harvard University Press.

National Academy of Education. 2005. *A good teacher in every classroom: Preparing the highly qualified teachers our children deserve*. Edited by Linda Darling-Hammond and Joan Baratz-Snowden. San Francisco: Jossey-Bass.

National Governors Association Center for Best Practices (NGA Center) and Council of Chief State School Officers (CCSSO). 2010. *Common core state standards for English language arts and literacy in history/social studies, science, and technical subjects*. Washington, DC: National Commission on Excellence in Education.

National Research Council. 2000. *Eager to learn: Educating our preschoolers*. Washington, DC: National Academy Press.

Paley, Vivian G. 1979. *White teacher*. Cambridge, MA: Harvard University Press.

———. 1981. *Wally's stories*. Cambridge, MA: Harvard University Press.

———. 1984. *Boys and girls: Superheroes in the doll corner*. Chicago: University of Chicago Press.

———. 1986. *Mollie is three: Growing up in school*. Chicago: University of Chicago Press.

———. 1988. *Bad guys don't have birthdays*. Chicago: University of Chicago Press.

———. 1990. *The boy who would be a helicopter*. Cambridge, MA: Harvard University Press.

———. 1992. *You can't say you can't play*. Cambridge, MA: Harvard University Press.

———. 1996. *Kwanzaa and me: A teacher's story*. Cambridge, MA: Harvard University Press.

———. 1997. *The girl with the brown crayon*. Cambridge, MA: Harvard University Press.

———. 1999. *The kindness of children*. Cambridge, MA: Harvard University Press.

———. 2001. *In Mrs. Tully's room: A childcare portrait*. Cambridge, MA: Harvard University Press.

———. 2004. *A child's work: The importance of fantasy play*. Chicago: University of Chicago Press.

———. 2010. *The boy on the beach: Building community through play*. Chicago: University of Chicago Press.

Provenzano, Eugene, and Arlene Brett. 1983. *The complete block book*. Syracuse, NY: Syracuse University Press.

Smilansky, Sara. 1968. *The effects of sociodramatic play on disadvantaged preschool children*. New York: John Wiley and Sons.

Sulzby, Elizabeth. 1985. "Children's emergent reading of favorite story books: A developmental study." *Reading Research Quarterly* 20 (4): 458–81.

Vivian Gussin Paley and the boy who could tell stories. 2002. Muncie, IN: The Child Care Collection at Ball State University, DVD.

Vygotsky, Lev. 1962. *Thought and language.* Cambridge, MA: MIT Press.

————. 1978. *Mind in society: The development of higher psychological processes,* edited by Michael Cole, Vera John-Steiner, Sylvia Scribner, and Ellen Souberman. Cambridge, MA: Harvard University Press.

————. 1981. "The genesis of higher mental functions." Pp. 144–88 in *The concept of activity in Soviet psychology,* edited by James V. Wertsch. New York: Sharpe, Armonk.

————. 1987. *The collected works of L. S. Vygotsky.* Vol. 1, *Problems of general psychology.* New York: Plenum Press.

Wertsch, James V., ed. 1981. *The concept of activity in Soviet psychology.* New York: Sharpe, Armonk.

Children's Books

Brown, Margaret Wise. 1975. *Goodnight moon.* New York: Harper and Row.

Burningham, John. 1970. *Mr. Gumpy's outing.* New York: Holt, Rinehart and Winston.

Carle, Eric. 1969. *The very hungry caterpillar.* New York: Penguin Putnam.

Ginsburg, Mirra. 1972. *The chick and the duckling.* New York: Simon and Schuster.

Isadora, R. 2007. *The twelve dancing princesses.* New York: G. P. Putnam's Sons.

Krauss, Ruth. 1945. *The carrot seed.* New York: Harper and Row.

Mayer, Mercer. 1968. *There's a nightmare in my closet.* New York: Dial Press.

————. 1976. *Liza Lou and the yeller belly swamp.* New York: Macmillan.

Sendak, Maurice. 1963. *Where the wild things are.* New York: Harper and Row.

Dr. Seuss. 1957. *The cat in the hat.* New York: Random House.

————. 1963. *Hop on pop.* New York: Beginner Books.

Index

WITHDRAWAL